Neither Cruel Nor Unusual

Neither Cruel Nor Unusual

FRANK G. CARRINGTON

ARLINGTON HOUSE·PUBLISHERS
NEW ROCHELLE, NEW YORK

Third printing, July 1979

Library of Congress Cataloging in Publication Data

Carrington, Frank.
    Neither cruel nor unusual.
    Includes index.
    1. Capital punishment—United States. I. Title.
HV8697.C35   364.6'6'0973   77-29122
ISBN 0-87000-405-0

Manufactured in the United States of America

To
FRED E. INBAU,
John Henry Wigmore Professor of Law
(Emeritus),
Northwestern University Law School,
who was speaking out for the victims
long before it became fashionable

Contents

Part III. THE SUPREME ARBITER: THE SUPREME COURT AND THE DEATH PENALTY

Foreword

Seldom in one's life does any person have the opportunity to come to grips directly with a moral issue of such lasting and universal impact as capital punishment—the exaction of human life by a political or religious entity for certain crimes, as that entity has defined them.

While murder, commencing—we are told—with the assault of Cain upon Abel, seems to be an indelible stain on the human condition, just and righteous people throughout history have tried through their ideals and actions to eradicate it. Except in a few isolated, arcadian, and now extinct cultures, they have failed.

Thus, we in mid-twentieth-century America find ourselves coping with this moral dilemma.

Do we accept the absolutes propounded in *Exodus*?

"Whoever strikes a man so that he dies shall be put to death."

"... if a man wilfully attacks another to kill him treacherously, you shall take him from my altar, that he may die."

"... you shall give life for life ..."

9

Or do we accept the conclusions of later religious and philosophical discourse:

a) that the state is bound as strictly as man to the Commandment (also from *Exodus*) that "Thou shalt not kill";

b) that no man or woman is intrinsically evil; only their actions may be evil; and each person has a potential for good that must be salvaged and developed; and

c) that the state, as the embodiment of a society's ideals and aspirations, must be above the sins of its constitutents and should set an example for its people as a paragon of those ideals.

All of these propositions are enticing. Each should be put into perspective.

For this reason, Frank Carrington's book should be read by all conscientious people. He pulls together an imposing collection of case histories, moral and legal arguments, and statistics to make *The Case for Capital Punishment.*

As I wrote in a letter to syndicated Columnist Jim Bishop a few years ago, it is a physically and intellectually wrenching experience to become a proponent of an act so solemn, so irrevocable, and so contrary to our best instincts as capital punishment.

I am squeamish over state-sanctioned killings, which is what executions are. But until mankind reaches a state of perfectibility I cannot now imagine, capital punishment must remain a finely honed scapel in society's surgical kit, to be used discreetly and as a last resort, for sure, but to be used unflinchingly when cancerous tissue of the Charles Manson—Richard Speck type, whose cases are covered in this book, infects our social body.

"What about the Judaeo-Christian tradition of mercy?" opponents ask.

The question betrays a misunderstanding of the word and the virtue it connotes.

You speak of mercy. Mercy has no meaning, no integrity if it is granted carte blanche. Mercy only becomes a reality and a virtue if we can say to a man or woman, "You have committed the highest crime against nature. You have killed another human being. But we realize that there were extenuating circumstances. Therefore, we grant you mercy. We grant to you

10

the privilege of continuing to live." It is not mercy—or justice—to cause a person who kills out of fear or heat of passion or frustration to be given the same punishment as Manson or Knowles or Richard Speck. That, as you must know, is more aptly described as travesty.

I wish you or I had a solution. But we don't. I wish tomorrow we could march with trumpets around the battlements of Raiford, Attica, and Soledad and bring the walls tumbling down. But we can't. And I wish we could put the ax to every gallows, electric chair, and gas chamber. But we can't. And until we have reached that elusive state of perfection we shall not be able to. In the meantime the best we can do to perpetuate our hope is to mete out justice, tempered by mercy.

After reading this excellent study by Frank Carrington, I think the reader will accept the conviction that I have adopted: *The human capacity for good and for compassion make the death penalty tragic; the human capacity for evil and depraved behavior make the death penalty necessary.*

ROBERT L. SHEVIN
Attorney General
State of Florida

Introduction

Unlike the introductions to most books, this one has been written as much to try to explain what the book is *not* about, as what it *is* about.

This book does not purport to be either a scholarly historical dissertation about capital punishment in the United States or a definitive legal treatise on the Eighth and Fourteenth Amendments to the Constitution of the United States, which prohibit cruel and unusual punishment by either the federal government or the several states. So many such books have been written that one who wished to digest them all to a point of complete comprehension would be hard pressed to do so in a lifetime of single-minded concentration.

Three considerations motivated this book:

1) For the past ten years capital punishment has been one of the most hotly contested political issues on the domestic scene;

2) During that same period there has been a fairly constant seesawing back and forth of victories and defeats for both

13

the proponents and the opponents of the death penalty; and,

3) Little of a concise nature has been written describing the ups and downs of the battle—and most certainly not from the perspective of the victims of crime.

The purpose of the book, then, is to look at the arguments advanced by both sides, the criminals and the victims; by the adversaries—those who girded for battle on either side; and, finally, how our criminal justice policy-makers—legislatures, courts, and, in the last analysis, the Supreme Court of the United States—chose to resolve the issues.

This book is written from the point of view of the proponents. It is not objective; it is a defense of the death penalty. In a prior book, *The Victims*, I took the position that it is high time that the rights of the victims of crime were recognized in our criminal-justice system. Nowhere is this more true than in the area of capital punishment. Richard Franklin Speck is today contentedly watching television in an Illinois penitentiary, at the taxpayers' expense. The eight student nurses whom he murdered have been in their graves for ten years, all but forgotten. There is an imbalance here that must be corrected, one that this book will address.

Part I

PERSPECTIVE

CHAPTER 1

They Won the Battle but They Lost the War

Gary Mark Gilmore is dead: the first man in this country to die by execution of judicial sentence in almost ten years.

They led the willing Gilmore into the cannery at Point of the Mountain Prison just after sunrise on January 17, 1977, and strapped him in a chair. His last words were "Let's do it," and they did it; he was executed by firing squad for the robbery-murder of Bennie Bushnell.

The event had all of the marks of high drama: the condemned man wanted to die; the American Civil Liberties Union, for reasons of its own totally unconnected with Gilmore's desires in the matter, did not want him to die. It had procured a last-minute stay of execution for him the night before the execution was scheduled, an effort that produced some pretty workmanlike cursing from the ungrateful Gilmore.

The attorney general of the state of Utah was not enthusiastic about the idea that the ACLU was going to determine criminal-justice policy in his state. He hopped a plane for Denver in the early morning hours of January 17 and got the United States Court of Appeals for the Tenth Circuit, sitting in extraordinary session, to overturn the stay. Events then proceeded on schedule.

The abolitionists—those who had been levying guerrilla warfare on the death penalty for the past ten years—pointed a trembling finger at Point of the Mountain and used such terms as "barbarism" and "brutalization"; the "floodgates," they predicted darkly, had been opened and we could now expect a "bloodbath."

Others took it more philosophically. The vast majority of students at Brigham Young University, the *New York Times* reported, "were relieved, satisfied, some even pleased that the convicted killer who murdered two of the University's students last summer was dead."[1] But they didn't go running around the streets of Provo driven by some sort of blood lust.

When the dust finally settled, one fact was clear. The moratorium was over. Capital punishment, after a decade of disuse (during which the number of murders in the United States had doubled), was once again, for better or worse, a reality.

The issue is certainly controversial. Intensely controversial. Men and women of otherwise tractable and agreeable disposition become steely-eyed and intransigent when the question of capital punishment crops up. Some—the abolitionists—swear that society has no right to take the life of any murderer,* no matter how villainous he may be; others—proponents of the death penalty—contend with equal fervor that society has not only the right, but the affirmative *duty*, to exact the supreme penalty from foul and vicious killers.

Capital punishment. The issue is a thorny one; and it goes

---

*This book deals with capital punishment for murder, which is the ultimate crime. Prior to June 29, 1977 some states had retained the death penalty for rape and other crimes. On that date, however, the U.S. Supreme Court held that the infliction of capital punishment was "disproportionate" to the offense of rape where no life had been taken. *Coker v. Georgia*, 97 S.Ct. 2861. I disagree with the decision; in some cases an aggravated rape can approach the viciousness and depravity of a murder. Nevertheless, since the Court has spoken, nothing is to be gained by rehashing the issue.

18

back to a time shortly after our nation was founded. As far back as 1792, one Benjamin Rush, an energetic and apparently influential Philadelphia physician, took it upon himself to call for an end to capital punishment because a sentence of life imprisonment held out the possibility of rehabilitation of the criminal.[2]

Dr. Rush was ahead of his time in seeking an end to the death penalty; abolitionist sentiment was unpopular then. Just three years earlier the framers of the Bill of Rights to the Constitution of the United States had expressly recognized capital punishment in the Fifth Amendment. Progressive as he was on the death penalty issue, Dr. Rush was standing in place when he talked about rehabilitation. Our society did not then know how to go about the business of rehabilitating lawless people, and it probably knows less about it today.* "There is no such thing as a bad boy" is a theory that simply has not worked.

Be that as it may, Dr. Rush's example drew adherents to the abolitionist cause. They were, we may presume, men of compassion and good will who set about to ensure that the truly depraved members of society, who were not men of compassion and good will, and who preyed most voraciously upon the innocent, should not be called upon to suffer the supreme penalty for their misdeeds.

The abolitionist cadre grew as the years passed, but it was always in the minority. To be sure, the abolitionists won a number of victories here and there. Several states abolished the death penalty; but, for the most part, the anti-capital-punishment forces were waging an uphill battle.

They ran up against the average citizen's old-fashioned commonsense view that if A murders B (and perhaps C, D, and E) in a particularly horrifying manner, then A should pay for B's life with his own; in order to punish him, to make sure that he does not kill someone else, and to deter others from following his example.

The abolitionists use terms like "barbarous" to describe the

*For example, Leonard Orland, professor of law at the University of Connecticut and a former member of the parole board of that state, wrote with admirable candor in the *New York Times* (September 24, 1971) that "in point of fact we are not even sure how to go about the task of rehabilitation."

theory of punishment, incapacitation, and deterrence, but it seemed to work. In the days when the death penalty was in effect, *and used*, we had fewer murders than we did when, after 1967, it fell into disuse. Many fewer.

The problem with the abolitionists is that they cannot or will not stand in the shoes of the victim. In fact, if you are arguing with a foe of the death penalty and you happen to mention the fact that perhaps murder *victims* have some bearing on the matter, your opponent gets snappish. "Look," he will say irritably, "executing the killer won't bring the victim back to life, so why talk about it?" Then he hits you with things like "the sanctity of human life" and the "human dignity" of the convicted murderer. Not the victim—the murderer. The abolitionists evidence a certain selectivity about the objects of their concern.

And that is where they made their mistake for so many years. The average citizen is not minded to become a killer; nor does he lose much sleep over the possibility of being falsely accused of murder, such situations being rare. What he *is* worried about is becoming a victim. As crime has proliferated in this country, the average citizen has watched the statistical chance of his becoming the victim of a violent crime grow drastically, and he doesn't like it.

Now this same citizen, distressed by the fact that his statistical chance of being murdered by a felon today is greater than the chance of a combat soldier being killed on the battlefields of World War II, goes out and votes for his national, state, and local legislators. These legislators, in turn, enact the laws that control our daily lives, including laws dealing with crime and punishment.

If an elected representative of the people wishes to remain one, he will generally reflect the will of his constituency. That is why the abolitionists struck out so many times in their efforts to do away with capital punishment through the legislative process. When the issue was put to the people, the response was, in most cases, "to hell with the likes of Speck, Manson, Starkweather, and Sirhan; we'll keep the gallows or the electric chair or whatever."

Frustrating. The abolitionists told themselves that they were right, that *they* were the oases of human kindness in the desert of a vindictive society; but the fact remained that those fools out there—the great majority of the electorate—kept beating them at the polls and putting hard-line boys in the state houses who refused to do the enlightened thing and knock off the death penalty.

Then someone in the abolitionist camp got smart. "Who is it," he said, "who is not responsible to public opinion, being appointed for life? And who is it who has the power to overrule any legislation, federal or state, based upon its interpretation of the United States Constitution?"

"Aha," came the rejoinder, "you're talking about the Supreme Court of the United States."

Precisely. So in the late sixties the battleground shifted. The abolitionists turned their energies away from the cave dwellers in Topeka, Springfield, and Austin and zeroed in on the big prize.

The tactic had another advantage. Once the lower courts learned that the Nine Men in Washington were taking an interest in the subject, stays of execution were not hard to come by, and no one was executed in the United States after 1967.

But nothing happened overnight. The abolitionists won a few preliminary legal skirmishes: jurors who had scruples against the death penalty could not automatically be excluded from sitting in capital cases[3] (which removed Richard Speck permanently from the shadow of the electric chair); statutes that permit the death penalty after a jury trial but not after a guilty plea are unconstitutional.[4] The Court was on the move in the capital punishment area and the abolitionists decided that it was really time to get down to cases.

Crafty as foxes, they waited for *the* case. They got it, or thought they had, when, in *Furman v. Georgia*,[5] the Court finally agreed to consider the question that had long intrigued the abolitionists: whether capital punishment is unconstitutional under the Eighth and Fourteenth Amendments to the Constitution of the United States.

The Court said yes on June 29, 1972. The abolitionist camp was elated. One writer who had worked long and hard for this victory describes it:

21

General disbelief. Numbness. Tears in people's eyes. Slowly smiles replaced gaping jaws; laughter and embraces filled the halls. "This place looks like we just landed a man on the moon," [abolitionist Douglas] Lyons shouted into a phone.[6]

They deserved their moment of joy; they had fought their battle with dedication and determination, occasionally with brilliance. But the merrymakers had not read the fine print in the opinion. The death penalty is unconstitutional *now*, the Court said in its razor-thin 5–4 opinion, BUT . . . "But" is an important word. The five-justice majority that held the death penalty unconstitutional (four justices held it to be constitutional) was divided.

Potter Stewart and Byron White, two of the majority justices, felt that capital punishment was not "cruel and unusual punishment" *per se*; rather, the capricious and arbitrary manner in which it was currently applied rendered it unconstitutional.

The majority of the Supreme Court, with one stroke of the pen, had wiped out capital punishment laws in 41 states; but they had not wiped out capital punishment forever.

The Court left open the question whether constitutional statutes *could* be written. It was willing to let the states have another crack at it.

That is exactly what 35 states and the federal government did. The news of the *Furman* decision had not been greeted in the statehouses across the nation with the same unbridled enthusiasm that the abolitionists accorded it. State legislators are proud men; they might concede that, as a matter of established principles of constitutional law, the Supreme Court has the power to override state legislation, but they don't like to be leaned on, and the wholesale nullification by the Court of death penalty laws in 41 states may fairly be called leaning. *

Nevertheless, many abolitionists believed that capital punishment was, as a result of the *Furman* decision, gone forever

---

*This was especially true since only three states and their capital punishment laws were represented before the Court. The other 38 states saw their good-faith legislative efforts thrown out without a hearing. This was done entirely legally, but it did not lead to a sweetening of relations between the legislative branch of government and the judiciary.

from the scene. They knew that there would always be a few super-hard-liners around to worry about, but in reality the matter was now foreclosed.

This sort of thinking was naive. The rapidity of the legislative response to *Furman* must have stunned even the most case-hardened abolitionist. The voters of the several states, fearful for the safety of their loved ones and themselves, were not about to shrug their shoulders and go on to nobler pursuits. Crime was on the rise—murder in particular—and great majorities of our citizenry were still adamantly insisting that something be done about the problem.

The solons got busy in Atlanta, Austin, Tallahassee, and elsewhere. Death penalty laws were passed by 35 states and the federal government, and then the proponents went back to the Supreme Court saying: "O.K. The ones we had before were unconstitutional. What about this batch?"

"Send them along," the Court said, "we'll have another look." The case of *Gregg v. Georgia*,[7] together with four comparison cases,[8] was heard in March of 1976. The abolitionists might have been forewarned of the result when Justice Lewis Powell, during the course of oral argument, asked pointedly how else we were going to deter the slaughter of Americans by murderers. Nor could they take a lot of comfort from the fact that Justice Harry Blackmun (personally an ardent foe of the death penalty) wondered aloud if anyone had given any thought to the victims of murderers.

Attempting to predict what the United States Supreme Court will do in a given case is an intellectual sport that is, roughly, as risky as is hang-gliding among the physical sports. Nevertheless, many Court-watchers felt that this time around, the good-faith efforts of the states to come up with something constitutional would receive a sympathetic hearing.

They did; at least partially. On July 2, 1976, a majority of the Court held that capital punishment statutes in Florida, Texas, and Georgia—statutes that provided for the fullest sort of legal determination of the question whether death was the appropriate penalty—were constitutional. Statutes in North Carolina and Louisiana, which made the death penalty mandatory, were struck down; a sop, perhaps, to the abolitionists.

The bottom line, however, was that Florida, Georgia, and

Texas were in compliance with the Constitution and they could, if they wished, dust off the long-unused electric chair. Not only that, the three statutes that were upheld could now become models for any state in the union that desired, constitutionally, to get on with the business of executing its murderers.

There wasn't much cavorting in the halls by the abolitionists when *Gregg* came down. Aryeh Neier, executive director of the American Civil Liberties Union, which had been in the forefront of the fight against capital punishment, noted the date of the decision and commented darkly that it was a hell of a way to run a Bicentennial celebration. Convicted murderers on death row in Texas, Florida, and Georgia understandably had a haunted look in their eyes when interviewed on network news.

The thing was done, though. The Court had spoken. *Furman*, which freed some 631 vicious men and women from the specter of execution, had been a temporary hiatus. *Gregg* closed the breach. Now society could again exact the supreme penalty. A collective sigh of relief went up from those who are more concerned with victims' rights than the rights of convicted murderers.

I had predicted the outcome. In *The Victims*, published a year earlier, I stated:

> In the *Furman* case the abolitionists may have won the battle and yet lost the war. As crime continues to rise, law-abiding citizens are reacting strongly to the permissiveness towards murderers embodied in *Furman*. There may be an equally strong reaction among state and national legislators to having the laws that they had in good faith enacted for the protection of the innocent, rendered impotent by the whimsical . . . judicial legislation of Justices Brennan, Douglas and Marshall.[9]

I hasten to add that no accolades for unusual perceptiveness should be accorded to this particular prediction. It was simply the way things were headed. The *kamikazes* of the abolitionist movement crashed into the immovable barrier of public opinion, which simply refused to tolerate the idea that lawbreakers could commit the most hideous crimes—murders for gain, murders in the commission of a felony, multiple murders, and so on—without any fear of the supreme penalty. And, as will be seen, the fact that public support for capital punishment could be demonstrated was important in the Supreme Court's decision in Gregg v. Georgia.

So the abolitionists won the battle in Furman and lost the war in Gregg. The following chapters will look at just how the battle was won by the proponents—and why.

Notes

1. Grace Lichtenstein, "Campus Where 2 Victims Studied Perceives Justice in the Execution," New York Times, January 18, 1977, p. 21c, col. 5.
2. Michael Meltsner, Cruel and Unusual, New York: Random House (1973), p. 48.
3. Witherspoon v. Illinois, 391 U.S. 510 (1968).
4. U.S. v. Jackson, 390 U.S. 570 (1968).
5. 408 U.S. 238 (1972).
6. Meltsner, op. cit., note 1, p. 290.
7. 428 U.S. 153 (1976).
8. Proffitt v. Florida, 428 U.S. 242; Jurek v. Texas, 428 U.S. 262; Woodson v. North Carolina, 428 U.S. 280; Roberts v. Louisiana, 428 U.S. 325 (1976).
9. Frank Carrington, The Victims, New Rochelle, N.Y.: Arlington House (1975), p. 187.

CHAPTER 2

The
Crime of Murder

Gary Mark Gilmore got a lot of ink prior to and just after his death. He deserved it. A convict on death row who wanted to die by a Utah firing squad, who raged at the American Civil Liberties Union and others for their unwanted efforts to spare his life, who mocked the security of the Utah State Penitentiary by making two near-successful suicide attempts through overdoses of drugs, and whose star-crossed lover, Nicole, almost joined him in one suicide pact (again unsuccessful), was a pretty newsworthy piece of goods.

There wasn't much question in most people's minds (nor, for that matter, in his own mind) that Gary Mark Gilmore should die. He had, after all, snuffed out the lives of two innocent people in the course of armed robberies.[1] On July 19, 1976, he robbed a filling station in Orem, forced the attendant, Max David Jensen, a law student with a wife and an infant daughter, to kneel on the bathroom floor, and then put two bullets into the back of the victim's head. The next night, he robbed a Provo motel, forced the night clerk, a young father named Bennie

Bushnell, to lie down, and again shot his victim in the head.*

Gary Mark Gilmore was no half-drunk card player who got into a cutting-scrape on Saturday night and, without really meaning to, killed someone. He was a cold-blooded butcher who deserved what he got. But, somewhat coincidentally, he shared the premises of the Utah State Penitentiary with two *former* death row inmates whose exploits make Gilmore's pallid by comparison. They are Myron Lance, 35, and Walter Kelbach, 38.

Everybody goes on a spree now and then; it's human nature.

Myron Lance and Walter Kelbach are only human; and they went on a little spree of their own just before Christmas of 1966 in Salt Lake City. They drank some beer, they popped a few pills—just a couple of good ole boys having some fun. And they left six corpses in their wake.

Lance and Kelbach will never be executed for what they did on their little romp. They were captured, to be sure, and tried and convicted, and sentenced to death under the state of Utah's unique plan whereby the condemned gets to elect whether to die by hanging or the firing squad. Beneficiaries of the United States Supreme Court's *Furman* decision, they were spared this election. Lance and Kelbach got a pass: three square meals a day, television, the hobby shop, and so on for the rest of their lives, or until they are paroled. They will never be begging for *their* lives as did one of their victims whom they butchered in the desert as they laughed "at the way he squirmed."

Now, that is a pretty heavy accusation to make. I mean, we know they *killed* their victims and all; but we weren't *there*. We can't actually *know* that they laughed at the way their victims squirmed, can we?

Well, as a matter of fact, we *do* know it because Lance and Kelbach told us so themselves. On the NBC television network.

The program was "Thou Shalt Not Kill,"[2] an hour-long documentary televised nationally on July 28, 1972,** in which Lance

*Gilmore was convicted only of the Bushnell slaying; he confessed to the Jensen murder as well.
**"Thou Shalt Not Kill" was filmed before the Furmam decision legislated capital punishment out of existence but was aired after the decision.

27

and Kelbach described for NBC news reporter Carl Stern just exactly what they did on their odyssey of murder, and how they felt about it.

In July of 1972 those preshow warnings to parents that they might want to keep their children from watching a particular program were relatively rare. Such warnings are commonplace now, as explicit depictions of violence and unnatural sex are being aired more and more on prime time; but back then, when the "voice-over"[3] told the adults that they had better pack the little ones off to bed if they didn't want a bunch of nightmares on their hands, it meant that some pretty unusual stuff was going to be shown.

There they were: Lance and Kelbach attired in their prison whites, along with Carl Stern looking properly serious. Myron Lance is a smirky little man with a shaved head. Kelbach, dark-haired with a hatchet-face, was the more voluble and apparently the leader of the two. It was a toss-up which was the more evil.

As the program opened, Lance and Kelbach mused about how much fun it would be to take a machine gun (or a tank) out onto a street and shoot people at random.

> KELBACH: You could see people scattering all over, windows breaking, people just falling down, blood running all over. It would be exciting.[4]

Exciting. But Carl Stern wasn't having too much of such speculation. He wanted to get down to the actual murders. Lance and Kelbach obliged.

Kelbach said that on the night of December 17, 1966, he and Lance robbed a filling station and then decided to take the attendant, 18-year-old Stephen Shea, along with them. They made him undress, put him in the back of their station wagon, and drove him out into the desert. On the way they discussed killing the terrified Shea, in his presence. They flipped a coin to see who would do the job.

Kelbach "won." He stabbed the victim repeatedly. Stern asked if the kid said anything.

> KELBACH: He says, "Oh my God, I got a wife."[5]

> LANCE: At the time we thought it was kind of funny, really,

because, well, everything we was really doing at the time we thought was funny. Every action or move you'd make, it seemed really funny to us. And I think one of us even commented on, "Did you see the way he squirmed? Wasn't that funny?"[6]

They did the same thing the next night. Gas station. Kidnap attendant. Out to the desert. In goes the knife (Lance this time). And more chuckles.

By the following Wednesday the pair had wearied of gas station attendants and their pleas for mercy. They varied their act by getting into a taxicab and shooting the driver, Grant Creed Strong, age 30, in the head.

LANCE (gleefully): . . . so then I just pulled the trigger and blood flew everywhere. Oh boy! I never seen so much blood.[7]

They got nine dollars.

The one-murder-at-a-time bit was beginning to pall. They left the dead cab driver and went to Lolly's Tavern in Salt Lake City's West Side district. They played a little pinball, robbed the bartender, and then, firing at random, fatally shot James Sizemore, 47, a navy veteran; Fred William Lillie, 20; and Mrs. Beverly Mace, 34. They wounded several others and left.

KELBACH: They still owe me a nickel from the pinball machine.[8]

All good things must come to an end, and they did for Lance and Kelbach later that night at a police roadblock featuring an officer with a shotgun and no apparent reluctance to use it. The two were taken, roughly, into custody.

Pretty graphic. The viewers were getting their money's worth. Then the inevitable question: How did Lance and Kelbach feel about their victims now?

If the proponents of rehabilitation—the "there's no such thing as a bad boy" school of thought—had any expectations of dewy-eyed and high-minded expressions of remorse from Lance and Kelbach, they had another thing coming. Lance, to his enduring credit, expressed some slight regret about killing Mrs. Mace, but that was about it:

29

LANCE: Other than that I haven't any real feelings towards any of the others—has no value.[9]

Kelbach was not about to plead to the charge of being wishy-washy, not even about the woman.

KELBACH: I got no feelings whatsoever. I got—I could be perfectly honest with ya, I'd have no feelings if somebody keeled over right here. I got—wouldn't make no difference to me really. I got no feeling about anything I've done.[10]

He elaborated further: "I don't mind people gettin' hurt because I just like to watch it."[11]

The efforts of the abolitionists have vindicated the human dignity and the sanctity of the lives of Myron Lance and Walter Kelbach.

There have been other sprees:

• Richard Franklin Speck, as stony-eyed and remorseless as Lance and Kelbach ever were, calmly and methodically murdered eight young student nurses in their Chicago townhouse in July of 1966. He was originally sentenced to death but the abolitionists got his life spared for him. Speck became eligible for parole in 1976, after serving nine years. Not surprisingly, it was denied; but if he continues to behave himself in prison, he will continue to be eligible and maybe someday . . .

• The Manson Clan. People have pretty much given up on trying to figure out just how many people they killed. Charles Manson and his "clan" members stood trial for ten of the killings; all were convicted and sentenced to die, but the abolitionists took care of *that* little matter, too. They prevailed on the California Supreme Court to hold that the death penalty was "cruel and unusual" punishment under the California constitution (the only state supreme court so to rule). *Everybody* in California prisons is eligible for parole after a maximum of seven years, so maybe someday . . .

• Charlie Starkweather and Caril Ann Fugate went on a little escapade across Nebraska in 1958 that left ten dead. Charlie was not as lucky as Speck and Manson. The abolitionists hadn't got their act together yet and he died in the electric chair. Caril Ann Fugate was paroled in 1976.

30

Speck, Manson, Starkweather. Millions and millions of words have been written about them, but we have never seen the face of murder up quite so close and with such clarity as when Lance and Kelbach appeared in "Thou Shalt Not Kill." NBC provided a great public service. It zeroed in for us on the kinds of people for whom death is the only proper penalty; for, as one writer has noted in describing the trail at Nuremberg of the Nazi war criminals:

> Men who plot to degrade, torture and kill human life, however insignificant in their eyes that life may be, must learn that their own life is no more valuable . . .[12]

Let's take a look at the crime of murder from the perspective of those who have the responsibility for defining which murders are punishable by death: the legislatures of the several states.

The Supreme Court told them in the *Furman* decision that perhaps there were classes of cases for which the supreme penalty might be exacted provided that the standards for the death sentence were carefully drawn and the penalty was not applied in an arbitrary and discriminatory manner. The legislators responded and, as noted in Chapter 1, thirty-five states had enacted death penalty laws by 1976. They sought to classify certain acts as justifying capital punishment. And, in *Gregg v. Georgia*, *Jurek v. Texas*, and *Proffitt v. Florida*,* they came up with classifications that passed constitutional muster in the Supreme Court.

Sample provisions of the laws of these three states will give us an idea of what capital murder can constitutionally consist of in the United States today; but the statutory provisions by themselves will merely be dry statements of the law unless they are fleshed out with cases—murder cases—that the provisions were designed for.

The cases to be described are not necessarily cases that arose in Georgia, Texas, or Florida after the statutes in those states were written. They have been selected more or less at random

*See Chapter 1, notes 7 and 8 for case citations.

31

from across the country to illustrate what capital murder is in the abstract, and *why* the states chose to define capital murder as they did. In sum, the following cases are examples of the types of murder that the people of the several states, speaking through their elected representatives, considered to be sufficiently horrifying to the mind of the average citizen (*nothing* seems to horrify the abolitionists) that death is the proper penalty.

The statutes of Florida,[13] Georgia,[14] and Texas[15] have this in common: first they prohibit willful and premeditated murder (and other crimes); next they provide a penalty of death or life imprisonment for those convicted of the crimes; and, finally, while they list a number of factors that will aggravate the offense sufficiently to require the death penalty, they also contain built-in safeguards to mitigate the offense or to provide for a judicial review of every death sentence so that the sentence is not improperly applied.

This is what the Supreme Court liked about the Georgia, Florida, and Texas statutes. There was no hard-and-fast rule; a certain amount of flexibility was built into each case by law. Courts and juries could look at *that* case in isolation and make decisions based on the facts of that particular case. The defendant would get his day in court, and a little more.

What kinds of murder did the legislators decide warranted the supreme penalty? What special facts were needed to aggravate a homicide into a capital homicide?

> GEORGIA: *The offense of murder,* rape, armed robbery, or kidnapping was outrageously vile, horrible, or inhuman in that it involved torture, depravity of mind, or an aggravated battery to the victims.*[16]

Like the crimes of Lance and Kelbach. If a legislator had any such crime in mind, it was theirs. But some of their colleagues have made their mark in the "vile, horrible, or inhuman" department too. Examples:

- *Boston, October 1973*. Rene Wagler, a 24-year-old carpen-

---

*As noted in Chapter 1, this book deals with the punishment for murder only and only murder cases will be described.

ter who chose to live in the ghetto because she sympathized with the people there, was carrying a two-gallon can of gasoline to her car, which had run out of fuel. Three young black men

> dragged her down the alley and into the yard. She was forced to pour the two gallons of gasoline she was carrying over herself. A match flickered in the dark, and Rene, her clothes and skin soaked with gasoline, was set on fire. Anyone who has seen Buddhist self-immolation on television will have some idea of what happens to the human body when it becomes a gasoline-soaked torch.[17]

- *Lakewood, California, July 1972.* Four-year-old Joyce Ann Huff was playing in her yard when a car approached, slowed down, and someone in the back seat took careful aim and shot the little girl to death with a shotgun. Three men were arrested. The one who was eventually convicted of this murder had an arrest record for attempted murder, assault with a deadly weapon, robbery, burglary, arson, and narcotics offenses. The killing occurred four days after the *Furman* decision had outlawed capital punishment.[18]
- In 1964 Dr. Geza De Kaplany, a physician in northern California, murdered his wife. He didn't just shoot her or whack her on the head; he brought his medical skills to bear on the matter. Mrs. Dianne Feinstein, a member of the San Francisco Board of Supervisors, wrote an angry piece for the *San Francisco Herald-Examiner* about the killing:

> De Kaplany, a physician, premeditated the murder of his wife. He assembled a lethal torture kit of three acids, strapped his beautiful 25-year-old wife to the bed, and for three hours mutilated and charred 60 percent of her body with acid.
>
> Her face was beyond recognition, ears and eyelids burned off, sight lost, breasts and genital areas mutilated.
>
> The prosecution asked for the death penalty because of the aggravated nature of the offense, which included torture and mayhem, and because of the intense suffering of the victim who lived for one month maimed and in terrible pain crying for the mercy of death.
>
> The jury sentenced De Kaplany to "life" after testimony that the case would be given a "special (public) interest" designation which would entitle it to special considera-

33

tion by the Adult Authority* whose nine members would sit "en banc" (as a whole) when they considered parole.[19]

Everything is relative in this life. Lance and Kelbach almost make Gary Mark Gilmore look good by comparison, and Dr. De Kaplany almost makes Lance and Kelbach look good—*their* victims only took minutes to die.

In consolation, can we feel fairly sure that after a crime such as his, Dr. De Kaplany won't see the outside for a good long while? Well, not exactly. The good doctor is currently practicing medicine in Taiwan after serving only 12 years. In a sneaky and shady deal, the California Adult Authority, *not* sitting as a whole as the jury that sentenced him required, freed De Kaplany and had him whisked out of the country before anyone knew anything about it. Take heart, Charlie Manson!

Whoever it was that wrote the provision of the Georgia law about vile, depraved, horrible, and inhuman murders may or may not have heard of the Wagler, Huff, or De Kaplany cases, but he knew what he was talking about.

> TEXAS: *The person intentionally committed the murder in the course of committing or attempting to commit kidnapping, burglary, robbery, forcible rape, or arson.*[20]

Felony murder. The thesis behind this provision is basically simple. The commission of felonies is a matter of free will. No one, for example, is forced to commit an armed robbery or a rape. If he elects to do so and is thereafter caught and convicted, we are going to send him away for a while (or so we hope). If, however, he decides to raise the ante and kill someone in the process—to keep the victim from testifying against him, or out of sheer maliciousness, or whatever—then *we* are going to raise the ante too, and we are going to execute him for it. The plea that "My client panicked and that's why he had to gun down the 70-year-old couple in the 'Mom and Pop' store he was robbing," simply won't wash anymore.

- *Gaston, Indiana, July 1974.* Lester French and Charles

---

*The Adult Authority is the California Parole Board.

Martin, parolees from the Indiana State Penitentiary for rape and burglary respectively, decided to commit an armed robbery. They did, and then they raised the ante.

In July 1974 Cathy Wylie, the eldest of five children, was 19 years old. She had graduated from high school in the spring of 1973. Her grandparents (Mrs. Wylie's parents) operated a small country store in Somerville, Indiana, several miles from Gaston. Mrs. Wylie's father died in early July 1974, and her mother insisted on reopening the store, against the advice of others in the family. Cathy, who had her own car, volunteered to help her grandmother in the store. On the afternoon of July 22, 1974, Cathy was sent by her grandmother to buy some food for the fish in an aquarium in the store. Cathy drove to the local pet store, found it closed, and returned to the family store. When she returned, she apparently failed to notice (or perhaps did notice) a car parked out front with one man in it. Cathy entered the store to find a second man holding her grandmother at gunpoint. Cathy told her grandmother to remain calm and do everything the man said. The robbery was completed. The robber ripped the phone from the wall, bound the grandmother, and took Cathy hostage, promising to release her at the county line.

That evening, in Madison County (next adjoining), after she had been raped and sexually tortured and mutilated, Cathy Wylie was thrown into the river. She was not quite dead, however, and regained consciousness. The two men scrambled down the riverbank and together held her head under water until she drowned.[21]

French and Martin are currently appealing sentences of death.

• *Chicago, December 1976.* Freddie Martin is presumably no kin to the Charles Martin noted in the previous example. He's as vicious, though. He just got 150–450 years in the Illinois State Penitentiary for murder. (He will be eligible for parole in eleven years and three months, being given credit for any time he spent in jail prior to his trial.)

Martin, a courageous individual, apparently selected his victims based on their age: the older the better. His first known robbery victim was an 85-year-old lady. On parole at the time

35

from burglary and narcotics convictions, he choked and robbed her. She lived, Freddie was caught and convicted, and did four years of a five-to-eighteen-year sentence.

Rehabilitated, according to the Illinois Parole Board, he was released in 1975. In short order he robbed, tortured, and murdered Gus Strombeck, 74, Edward Mullen, 86, and Herbert Alferrink and his wife, 76 and 77 respectively.[22]

This modern-day Robin Hood (he steals from the old, gives to himself) was expressionless during court proceedings until he was sentenced. Then he smiled. He can count, and eleven years and three months subtracted from 150 to 450 is . . . The judge said that he wished Illinois had the death penalty but it didn't.* Martin just smiled; in eleven years and three months he will be 39, and there will be plenty of the over-70 generation around then.

• *Grandin, Missouri 1973.* Two men wired up Robert Kitterman with dynamite and extorted $9,811 from his family-owned bank, then they took Kitterman, his wife Bertha, and their 17-year-old daughter Roberta out into the woods. They tied their wrists to trees with nylon cords and killed each of them with one shot in the back of the head.[23]

The *St. Louis Globe-Democrat* ran a grisly photograph of the bodies hanging from the trees, and editorialized:

> The photograph tells more graphically than any words how abominably cruel and heartless were the [Kitterman murderers].
> The Kittermans never had a chance. The slayers kidnapped the mother and daughter, and then killed all three when Mr. Kitterman came to the scene to pay the ransom. They tied the three Kittermans to the trees like animals and shot each in the head.[24]

The editorial called for a return of the death penalty in Missouri. Undoubtedly a lot of abolitionists read the editorial and, characteristically, deplored it. While deploring it, they may or may not have had to turn their eyes away from the accompanying photograph of three bodies slumped to the ground, their wrists firmly bound to the trees at about waist level.

---

*Illinois had enacted a death penalty law after the *Furman* decision but the Illinois Supreme Court struck it down.

● *Bellevue, Iowa, 1969.* Sixty-year-old police chief Earl Berendes was investigating a break-in at a garage. He was beaten to death with a shovel. The autopsy indicated that Chief Berendes died of massive skull injuries. Two men and a woman were charged with the crime.

On October 3, 1969, after pleading guilty to second-degree murder, one of the trio of suspects, William P. Sweeney, 25, was sentenced to 75 years in prison for his part in Chief Berendes' killing. The other man received the same sentence and the woman was placed on probation. On June 12, 1972, having served two years and nine months of his sentence, Sweeney was released on parole by the Iowa Parole Board.[25]

The citizens of Bellevue were understandably upset over this example of leniency to one convicted of murdering their police chief. According to the *Des Moines Register* of June 14, 1972, Mayor Kenneth Kell and the Bellevue City Council sent letters of complaint to the governor of Iowa and to the Iowa Parole Board. Jack Bedell, a member of the parole board, replied to their complaints. According to the *Register*, Bedell airily explained that the board's decision was based on the recommendation of the institutional staff. The recommendation stated that the time was ripe to release Sweeney if they "expected a complete rehabilitation," and that "our only excuse for keeping him incarcerated any longer would have been just to punish him. And to keep him only to punish him is not in keeping with the attitude of correcting."

GEORGIA: *The offense of murder was committed against any peace officer, corrections employee or fireman while engaged in the performance of his duties.*[26]

Novelist Dame Rebecca West pretty well summed up the rationale for this provision:

As for the murder of law enforcement officers and prison guards, it is unrealistic for society to raise and maintain organizations in order that they might protect it from vio-

37

lence without giving these organizations protection from
the violent men they will be obliged to confront.[27]

Why is it that the British have such a facility for getting right
to the heart of the matter and stating it so succinctly? Miss West
lucidly defines the problem: we do raise and maintain organizations to protect us—police, corrections, and firefighters—and
we tell them to shield us from violent criminal offenders on the
street, from the same criminals when they are behind bars, and
from the ravages of fire. We have a definitive obligation to protect them, too.

Being a policeman is no easy job. He is the principal target
of assault by any ding-a-ling who happens to resent authority.
Ninety-three law enforcement officers were murdered in the
first ten months of 1976, according to the FBI. Of the victims,
24 were attempting arrests for crimes other than robbery or burglary, 17 were handling disturbance calls, 13 were ambushed,
13 were dealing with robberies, nine were making traffic stops,
nine were investigating suspicious persons, five were investigating burglaries, two were handling deranged persons, and
one was handling a prisoner.[28]

Some of the abolitionist cadre, specifically the American
Civil Liberties Union, will fight with the ferocity of a cornered
wolverine to spare the life of an individual who has, say, shot
a policeman to death from ambush. These same ACLU zealots
are equally quick to condemn any use of force by the police in
their own defense. Criminals' rights: 100 percent; the safety of
law enforcement officers: absolute zero.

• *Omaha, August 1970.* David Rice, Duane Peak, and Edwin
Poindexter didn't like cops. As officials of the Omaha Committee to Combat Fascism, an offshoot of the Black Panther Party,
they publicly called for the murder of policemen. Omaha not
being exactly a hotbed of radicalism, the public was slow in responding to the suggestion, so Messrs. Rice, Peak, and Poindexter took matters into their own hands.

They constructed a booby-trap-type dynamite bomb, placed
it in a suitcase, and set the suitcase in a vacant house. They
then placed an emergency call to the police. Officer Larry
Minard was one of the policemen responding to the call. He
was blown to bits; two other officers were injured.

38

This was a pretty hideous ambush murder. It resulted in a life sentence for David Rice, who built the bomb, and in whose house the police found dynamite and other paraphernalia that were traced directly to the bomb itself.

Ironically, David Rice was almost set free. The Nebraska Supreme Court upheld his conviction, but the federal courts found that the search of Rice's house that turned up the dynamite was "illegal." Fortunately, Nebraska took the case to the U.S. Supreme Court.

During oral argument, Chief Justice Warren Burger asked Rice's defense counsel whether he thought the convicted murderer by dynamite of a policeman should go scot-free because of a technical search-and-seizure violation.

"Yes," said the ACLU attorney, giving a pretty good idea of how much value the leading abolitionist organization places on a policeman's life.

"No," said the Court some months later in an opinion affirming Rice's conviction.[29] It told the lower federal courts that it was not their business to reverse en masse state supreme court decisions about searches and seizures.

The Florida, Georgia, and Texas death penalty statutes that the Supreme Court upheld all prescribe the supreme penalty for the murder of a law enforcement officer. The legislators placed a premium on the lives of the men in the thin blue line that separates the rest of us from the lawless and violent. "If you kill a cop, we'll kill you," they say.

That sort of troglodyte thinking does not sit well with the members of the Maryland ACLU who, incredibly, went to court to *defend* the right of citizens to call for and blueprint the ambush murder of policemen.

• *Baltimore, 1970.* It was the height of the time of rebellion. "Kill the pigs!" was quite a fashionable slogan. The Black Panther Party went a step further. It distributed throughout the city of Baltimore hate literature that explicitly urged the murder of policemen and contained a detailed plan of the best way to ambush a police car with rifle fire. Lo and behold, someone did just that; following the plan to the letter, he killed one officer and wounded another.

Baltimore City Police Commissioner Donald D. Pomerleau is not a man to be trifled with in the best of times. He saw red at

39

the murder of one of his officers and went to court to seek an injunction againt the Black Panthers to halt further distribution of their blueprint for murder.[30]

The ACLU leaped into the fray, on the side of the Panthers of course. "You can't enjoin the advocacy and instruction of how to murder police officers," they told the court. "Why, that's free speech!"

"I can. And I'm going to," retorted the court, with some pretty tart remarks comparing the Panthers' hate campaign against the Baltimore city police to that of Hitler against the Jews in the 1930s.

The life of the average correctional officer is no bed of roses either. He is locked up, on a day-to-day basis, with inmates who are in prison precisely because they are bad people. Adding to the problems of the professional correctional people are the efforts of any number of busybodies who, perhaps wearying of Save the Trees or some such crusade, have made "prisoners' rights" their next quest for the Holy Grail.

The courts, especially the federal courts, haven't helped much. Judges have intervened in the business of running prisons in a big way, and while some conceded abuses have commendably been corrected, we don't need decisions such as the one in which a judge ordered a warden to make available to a convicted burglar, serving time, two books: one dealt with picking locks, the other told how to make bombs.[31]

This new "free spirit" approach to corrections increases the danger to prison guards and others who work behind the walls. In California alone, between 1970 and 1973, eleven prison staff members were murdered by inmates.[32] A lifer, or a convict doing a pretty stiff jolt, has little incentive not to kill a guard if the spirit happens to move him. But if he knows that the electric chair or the gas chamber is waiting for him at the end of the hall, he may think twice.

Finally, firemen: that courageous group of men who face different but still appalling dangers for the protection of others. Fortunately for them, there seems to be less of an authoritarian image about firefighters than about the police, and with the exception of some sniping during inner-city riots, they are less likely to be targets. Nevertheless, the thrust of the statute is to

40

give some added measure of protection to our protectors, and it is entirely proper that firefighters be included.

> GEORGIA: *The offense of murder was committed by a person in, or who has escaped from, the lawful custody of a police officer or a place of lawful confinement.*[33]

The reasoning behind this provision is straightforward: if somebody is already in a penal institution, he is there, in most cases, because he is dangerous and creates a menace to society by being at large. Furthermore, with the exception of certain minimum-security facilities from which prisoners can (and often do)* walk away, prisons are made for the purpose of confinement. They are not meant to be broken out of. Therefore the process of escape, by definition, carries with it a certain element of danger to the corrections officials who are there to prevent the breakout and to law enforcement officers whose job it is to recapture the escapee.

Legislatures that have enacted similar provisions are merely recognizing the fact that escapees and would-be escapees are dangerous and desperate men; if their desperation to escape, or to avoid capture, carries them to the point of murder, they're going to get knocked for it—and hard.

• *Flint, Michigan, April 1974.* Two men escaped from the prison farm at Marquette, Michigan. They then abducted a 34-year-old waitress from a Marquette restaurant and, when she tried to escape in a field near Oshkosh, Wisconsin, shot her to death in a fusillade of gunfire. They then blasted a Troy, Michigan policeman with shotguns as he surprised them during a filling station break-in. They were recaptured in Flint, two murders too late.[34]

On occasion, incarcerated criminals escape in order to take revenge on people against whom they hold a grudge.

• *Erath County, Texas, August 1974.* Dalton Williams carried

---

*Such an institution is the School for Boys at Lookout Mountain, Colorado. The hardened juvenile criminals there know that once they walk away, they can do pretty much what they want as far as crime is concerned and get nothing more added to their original sentence. The situation got so bad that one Colorado legislator facetiously suggested that the Department of Highways erect "Caution: Prisoners Escaping" signs on the highways around the school, much as "Deer Crossing" signs are used in wooded game areas.

a grudge. W. T. Baker, an otherwise inoffensive Texas rancher, had earlier testified against him. Williams and several other convicts escaped from the Colorado State Penitentiary and proceeded to Baker's ranch. They hid in the grass until Baker appeared on the porch of his home, then shot him four times with a .308 magnum rifle. Williams went up on the porch where the rancher was lying in a pool of blood, still alive, looked at him and asked him if he recognized him. Baker nodded. "I want you to know why I killed you," Williams said. "I told you I was going to do it." Williams and his fellow escapees then murdered Baker's wife.[35]

Dalton Williams is a single-minded individual who accomplishes whatever it is he sets out to do. If he were an advertising executive, he would probably have the General Motors account. But he isn't. His goal was to escape from prison, go to Texas, and murder Mr. Baker. He did it; and there is simply no reason in the world why he shouldn't die for it in the electric chair. If he doesn't, he may conjure up some new grudge against someone else, escape again (he has proved that he is perfectly capable of doing *that*), and blow away another innocent victim.

> FLORIDA: *The defendant knowingly created a great risk of death to many persons.*[36]

• *Madison, Wisconsin, August 1970.* Karleton Armstrong didn't like the military. The mathematics department at the University of Wisconsin did some work for the military. Karleton Armstrong blew up the mathematics building. A blow for freedom. Q.E.D.

One thing, though. Robert Fassnacht, a 33-year-old physicist, father of three children, happened to be in the building and Karleton blew him up, too. After a couple of years as a fugitive, Karleton was captured and pleaded guilty to second-degree murder.

Well, he wasn't going to be executed for his crime in any event because Wisconsin doesn't have the death penalty, but this fact wasn't enough for Daniel Ellsberg, the admitted thief of the Pentagon Papers. He wanted Karleton *cut loose* and he showed up at the sentencing hearing to tell the judge that that was what he wanted.

42

Prattling about the need to move toward a "just society," Ellsberg told the court that "the place to start is not by punishing the action of Karleton Armstrong."[37] You know, you can't make an omelette without breaking a few eggs.

The judge said, "Yes . . . well," and sentenced the bomber to 23 years in the penitentiary. Karleton was lucky. If he had carried out his peace mission in Florida or any other state with the "grave danger" capital-murder provision, he could have been (and certainly should have been) executed.

Bombs are like bombers. They have no conscience. They just go off and anybody within range gets it. Jerry Della Femina, a New York advertising executive, heartbreakingly described how his three-year-old daughter Jodi had just been grievously injured by a terrorist bomb blast in Manhattan:

> I am writing this column at 4 A.M. while sitting in a waiting room at New York Hospital. Inside, about 50 feet away, my three-year-old daughter, Jodi, is sleeping in a crib with both of her hands tied to her sides to keep her from touching the 100 stitches she has in her face. You see, Jodi made a terrible mistake a few hours ago. Almost a fatal mistake.
> She trusted the world of grownups.
> Like a million other three-year-olds all over the world, she took her mother's hand and walked with her to go out and play in the park. They walked past a building where a young militant had just placed a 15-inch pipe bomb. I guess it was bad timing on Jodi's part because she passed the building at the same time the bomb went off.
> The blast sent a rain of jagged glass into her tiny face. Now we all know that the militant didn't set out to injure Jodi. No. What he was looking for was "justice." My little girl just got in his way. And I'm sure that some people will tell you that Jodi being a three-year-old member of the establishment was at fault. Because when a man is looking for "justice" or looking to right the wrongs of the world with a bomb, it's your fault if you get in his way. The Mark Rudds of this world will tell you that the man who placed the bomb that went off in Jodi's face was merely defending himself from society, merely choosing his way to be heard and listened to.
> The Angela Davises of the world might tell you that three-year-old Jodi is just paying "dues" for several hundred years of oppression.
> The Eldridge Cleavers of this world might tell you that Jodi is only an early casualty of the war that's coming be-

tween the races. As I said before, there are a lot people who can give you a lot of good reasons, they say, for throwing bombs, and killing cops, and burning, and rioting, and looting and hating.

Just before I sat down to write this I walked into Jodi's room to check and see if she was asleep. I guess I made a little too much noise and I woke her. She smiled with her ripped-up lips and said, "Daddy, I ran and I fell."

You see, Jodi, being only three, doesn't know what a bomb is or what it does. She still thinks she fell and cut herself. For a second, I wanted to explain to her what had happened and then I realized how ridiculous it was and so I did something I haven't done since I was a little kid. I cried.

How do you tell a kid that a man took dynamite and buckshot and made a bomb that blew up and ripped your face? He did it in the name of "justice" and "freedom."

How do you explain?

Maybe the Mark Rudds or Angela Davises or Eldridge Cleavers of this world can explain to Jodi why her face had to be ruined this morning in the name of "justice."

Because, God knows, I can't.[38]

Jodi lived and, all things considered, came out of her ordeal pretty well after plastic surgery; no thanks, of course, to those who set the bomb.

That is what the legislators meant when they made capital a murder that is caused by an act that put many people in grave danger. The bomber, the arsonist, the skyjacker all fit within the definition of capital murderers if a death results, and well they should.

> GEORGIA: *The offender committed the offense of murder for himself or another, for the purpose of receiving money or any other thing of monetary value, like insurance.*[39]

• *Alta Loma, California, 1964.* Mrs. Lucille Miller was convicted of drugging her husband with nembutal and, while he was still alive, burning him to death in their car. Her conviction was affirmed by the California Court of Appeals, which commented rather pointedly in its opinion about her possible motive (in addition to the fact that she was having an affair with another man):

Dr. Miller had considerable life insurance, including double indemnity, payable to his wife, of which defendant had knowledge. Although his practice of dentistry was fairly successful, netting approximately $25,000 yearly before taxes, the Millers had debts of $64,000, of which $30,000 was attributable to the recent construction of their new home, the building of which the doctor did not favor, although he went along with it to keep peace in the family.[40]

Mrs. Miller received a life sentence but she was promptly released after serving the seven-year minimum term for murder in California.

And then there are the killers for hire.

• *Coeur D'Alene, Idaho, 1976.* "You earned your fee," stated the judge as he sentenced Philip Lindquist to death by hanging.

Lindquist had been convicted of murdering a woman who had been five months pregnant for a fee of $3,500. The victim's husband admitted that he had hired Lindquist, through an intermediary, to kill his wife in order to collect on a $60,000 insurance policy.[41]

The foregoing examples have been set forth to demonstrate: a) the classes of murders that state legislators have defined as punishable by death, and b) the complete depravity of the persons who commit such murders.

The abolitionists will almost assuredly characterize this chapter as nothing but a bunch of irrelevant "horror stories" designed to create passion and hatred against the likes of Lance and Kelbach, Freddie Martin, Dr. De Kaplany, and Dalton Williams.

Dean E. Donald Shapiro of the New York Law School, for example, takes the view that

> most of the arguments in favor of capital punishment have been primarily based on appeals to raw emotion and grounded in a lynch-mob psychology.[42]

I think it is time to examine such accusations more closely. First the old "lynch-mob psychology" ploy. This is nothing more than a neat bit of McCarthyism from the left: taking an opprobrious generalization and shotgunning it at anyone who holds a certain set of views.

Every sensible person in this country abhors lynchings. The word conjures up the picture of unfortunates who may or may not have been guilty of crimes but who certainly were not accorded due process of law, dangling from trees while a grinning crowd of men, women, and even children mill about below.

"Lynch-mob justice" is horrible, terrifying. Yet Dean Shapiro tars anyone who advocates capital punishment with the "lynch mob" brush. This is an astounding leap of logic. Lynching is, by definition, the *extrajudicial murder* of someone suspected of a crime, usually by a mob. Proponents of capital punishment have never called for this; rather, they call for *judicial execution*, under the law, of persons *proven guilty beyond a reasonable doubt* of one or more heinous and inhuman crimes.

I have never heard *one* advocate of the death penalty call for anything even remotely approaching "lynching,"* and neither, I suggest, has Dean Shapiro; yet he is pleased to sling the term at us. Pretty shoddy.

I categorically reject the "lynch mob" appellation. And I do not envision the 65 percent of our citizens who favored capital punishment in a recent poll, the two-to-one majorities of the voters in Illinois and California who voted to retain or restore the death penalty, or the legislators of 35 states as a huge mob, grinning and milling around under that tree.

Now to the old chestnut about the proponents' "appeals to raw emotion." Unlike the "lynch mob" accusation, which is a base lie, there is some truth to this; but the idea that the advocate of a particular point of view cannot appeal to the emotions of his listeners is patently ridiculous.

Murder is an emotional question. We're not talking about a bond issue to repair cracked sidewalks in Neenah, Wisconsin; we're talking about the willful taking of a human life. It happened some 20,000 times in this country last year. To tell the

---

*Proponents of capital punishment include the majority of law enforcement officers in this country, men who have vigorously prosecuted lynch mobs. For example, there was no more avid advocate of the death penalty than the late J. Edgar Hoover. Yet he marshaled the considerable resources of the Federal Bureau of Investigation to bring to justice the terrorists in the Deep South who were lynching blacks and civil rights workers.[43]

proponent of capital punishment that he must divorce all emotional references from his argument is roughly like telling someone who is pushing the use of seat belts that he must not mention automobile accidents.

Let's analyze the "appeal to raw emotion" argument. First, I don't know the difference between "raw" emotion and some other kind of emotion. I will let that pass.

Next, as best I can make out, when Dean Shapiro castigates an "appeal to the emotions," what he means is that he doesn't want to hear anything about the victims of murder—*nothing,* period! This is standard abolitionist dogma and it *has* to be, because if it weren't for the plight of the innocent victims, there would be no hue and cry for the death penalty. Suppose, for example, that the *only* murders committed in the United States were gangland-style slayings a la Buggsy Siegel's classic statement: "We only kill each other." The abolitionists would have a field day and the proponents' response would be a "ho hum" or, at best, perhaps a facetious suggestion that some sort of bounty system be set up to encourage the killing of mobsters by other mobsters.

But such is not the case. Most of our murder victims are totally innocent, and *that* is why the abolitionists don't want to hear about them. For two reasons: first, because, as I noted earlier, the average citizen identifies with the victim (as well he should, given his statistical chances of becoming one); and, second, when we describe, graphically, what happened to the victim, we of necessity point out the depravity of the murderer. This is the last thing the abolitionist wants to be reminded of, but it is what spurs the men and women in our state legislatures to vote "aye" when the capital punishment issue comes before them.

To the abolitionist, the statement that "Dr. Geza De Kaplany, who may have been responsible for the death of his wife 12 years ago, was released from prison today" would be a fine, unemotional account of the case. I am certain that Dean Shapiro would consider Dianne Feinstein's article (see pages 33–34), which described how De Kaplany tied his wife to the bed, burned out her eyes, her breasts, genitals, and 60 percent of her body with acid, and how she lingered for a month crying for the release of death, the rankest kind of emotional appeal. Well, it is. But what is wrong with that? The people of the state of California have a right to know about the antics of the Adult Authority and just exactly what the killer it surreptitiously freed did to his victim. They should bear this incident in mind if they are ever again called on to vote on the issue of capital punishment.*

Take another example. Reprinted here in full is the editorial from the *St. Louis Globe-Democrat*, mentioned earlier, that appeared with a photograph of the bodies of the Kitterman family, murdered and hanging by their wrists from trees:

Must Restore Death Penalty
GHASTLY, COLD-BLOODED CRIME

The accompanying picture is shocking and horrifying. It shows how three members of the Kitterman family of Grandin, Mo.—a daughter, Roberta, and Mr. and Mrs. Robert R. Kitterman—were brutally slain in a wooded area near Grandin.

The photograph tells more graphically than any words how abominably cruel and heartless were the killers of the Southeast Missouri banker, his wife, and their 17-year-old daughter.

The Kittermans never had a chance, The slayers kidnapped the mother and daughter, and then killed all three when Mr. Kitterman came to the scene to pay the ransom. They tied the three Kittermans to trees like animals and shot each in the head.

This immensely stark and tragic picture should convince everyone how urgently necessary it is to restore the discipline of the death penalty in Missouri and throughout the country.

It is possible that Roberta, Bertha, and Robert Kitterman would still be alive today if the nation had not yielded to the jello-brained bleeding hearts who think that even the kind of executioners who killed the Kitterman family can be reconstructed.

The only way society can protect itself against more such hideous crimes is to put those who commit them to death.

But to be an effective deterrent, the death penalty must be used. Those who are sentenced to death for capital crimes must be executed within a reasonable length of

*They retained it by a two-to-one vote in 1972 in a state-wide referendum.

time. As it is, not a single death sentence has been carried out in the United States since 1967.

The death penalty is further warranted because it is the only practical way to make certain that a murderer will not repeat his crime. Under today's permissive, revolving-door justice, it is almost an everyday occurrence to read where a convicted murderer, after serving a relatively short sentence, has killed again.

It has become increasingly obvious that criminals such as those who assassinated the Kitterman family have absolutely no fear of the law. If they had feared the consequences of their acts, they would not have dared to so much as put a finger on the Kittermans. Instead, they must have decided they could kill them—in order to keep them from being witnesses—and get away with it.

It is up to all Missourians who want to put a stop to these unspeakable crimes to demand that the General Assembly revise state laws on the death penalty so that capital punishment can be reinstituted.

Many legislatures across the country are moving to restore the death penalty and Missouri should waste no time doing likewise.[44]

Now I am going to concede to Dean Shapiro that this is an appeal to the emotions (probably to the "raw" ones, whatever that may mean). The picture, the graphic description of the suffering of the victims, and the depravity of the killers inflame us with anger. The editorial called for a return of the death penalty and the Missouri legislature *did* restore capital punishment, a fact for which the editorial writer can perhaps take considerable credit.

What I will *not* concede is that the picture and editorial should not have been run because they frankly appeal to one's emotions. Setting aside First Amendment freedom of speech issues (and I would assume that Dean Shapiro is a foe of censorship in other areas), I cannot for a moment believe that the editorial and picture should have been replaced with a short announcement that "the Kitterman family bank will not be open today because of a death in the family." And this is precisely what would be left to print if we were to sanitize the story so as to rid it of any emotional content.

I am unashamedly in the camp of Mrs. Feinstein and the *St. Louis Globe-Democrat*, and if I am accused of telling "horror stories," so be it. They *are* "horror stories"—stories of the horror of the sufferings the victims went through and stories of the horror of a society that permits murderers to roam around pretty much at will.

If the cases that I have described were isolated instances, I could, and should, be accused of distorting the issue. But they are not. Pick up any newspaper in any major urban area and you will find a new tale of a multiple slaying, a torture murder or rape murder, a murder in the course of another felony, or the slaying of a policeman. Multiply the cases I have described here by, say, a factor of a thousand. Then we may begin to get some sort of picture of the crime of murder.

Notes

1. Peter Goldman, et al., "Death Wish," *Newsweek*, November 29, 1976, p. 26, col. 1.
2. Peter Jeffries, producer and writer, "Thou Shalt Not Kill," NBC News, air date July 28, 1972, 9:30 P.M. EST. From the script.
3. *Ibid.*, p. 1.
4. *Ibid.*, p. 3.
5. *Ibid.*, p. 15.
6. *Ibid.*
7. *Ibid.*, p. 35.
8. *Ibid.*, p. 50.
9. *Ibid.*, p. 69.
10. *Ibid.*, p. 70.
11. *Ibid.*, p. 72.
12. Barrie Pitt, introduction to Leo Kahn, *The Nuremberg Trials*, New York: Ballantine Books (1973), p. 7.
13. Fla. Stat. Ann. ch. 782.04, 921.141 (Cum. Supp. 1975-1976).
14. Ga. Code Ann. ch. 26-3102, 27-2528, 27-2534.1, 27-2537 (Supp. 1975).
15. Vernon's Tex. Pen. Code Ann. ch. 19-03(a)(1974).
16. Ga. Code Ann. ch. 2534.1(b)(2).
17. Ted Morgan, "Remembering Rene," *New York Times Magazine*, November 11, 1973, p. 16.
18. "Police Arrest 3 for Shotgun 'Joy' Killing of Girl, 4," *Chicago Tribune*, July 5, 1972, p. 1.
19. Dianne Feinstein, "Life Prison Sentence That Would Mean No Parole," *San Francisco Herald-Examiner*, March 12, 1976, p. 35, col. 1.
20. Tex. Pen. Code ch. 19.02(a)(2)(1974).

21. Interview with Mrs. James Wylie, December 18, 1975.
22. Roger Simon, "The Crimes of Freddie Martin," *Chicago Sun-Times*, December 3, 1976, p. 1, col. 1.
23. "3 in Family Kidnapped, Slain in Extortion Plot," *Chicago Daily News*, January 18, 1973, p. 2, col. 2.
24. "Ghastly, Cold-blooded Crime," *St. Louis Globe-Democrat*, January 19, 1973, p. 12A, col. 1.
25. Thomas Ryder, "Paroled in '69 Killing; Jailed," *Des Moines Register*, December 22, 1972, p. 1.
26. Ga. Code Ann. ch. 2534.1(b)(8).
27. Rebecca West, "Capital Punishment, *New York Times*, April 1, 1973, Op. Ed. page.
28. "Police Deaths and Bomb Reports," *Crime Control Digest*, November 22, 1976, p. 3, col. 1.
29. *Wolff v. Rice*, 44 *U.S. Law Week* 5318 (1976).
30. *Pomerleau v. Black Panther Party*, Baltimore City Circuit Court, April, 1970.
31. "Unmanageable Jails in 10 Years Predicted," *Chicago Daily Law Bulletin*, July 5, 1974.
32. Earl Caldwell, "California Planning Tough Measures to Curb Violence in Penal Institutions," *New York Times*, January 14, 1974, p. 30.
33. Ga. Code Ann. ch. 2534.1(b)(9).
34. "Escaped Cons Seized, Linked to Two Killings," *Chicago Daily News*, April 22, 1974, p. 1, col. 5.
35. "Captured Convicts Tell of Killing Spree," *Chicago Tribune*, August 28, 1974, p. 1.
36. Fla. Stat. Ann. ch. 782.04, 921.141(c) (Supp. 1976-1977).
37. William Farrell, "Peace Activists Defend Bomber," *New York Times*, October 25, 1973, p. 9.
38. Jerry Della Femina, "The Bombing," *Marketing Communications*, October 1971, p. 17.
39. Ga. Code Ann. ch. 2534.1(b)(4).
40. *People v. Miller*, 245 C.A. pp. 2d 112 at page 124.
41. Associated Press dispatch, March 24, 1976.
42. E. Donald Shapiro, "Death Penalty . . . A Debasement of Morals," *Wall Street Journal*, December 9, 1976, p. 20, col. 6.
43. See Don Whitehead, *Assault on Terror: The FBI Against the Klan in Mississippi*, New York: Funk and Wagnalls (1970).
44. *St. Louis Globe-Democrat*, *loc. cit.*

CHAPTER 3

The Penalty for Murder

Civil libertarians are big on Thomas Jefferson, as well they should be. He was the intellectual force behind, and the chief architect of, the Bill of Rights: the first ten amendments to the Constitution of the United States. Indeed, it was Jefferson who, in 1789, hustled James Madison off to New York to ram the Bill of Rights through the First Continental Congress of the United States, a task that Madison accomplished with little difficulty.

Jefferson was probably a "liberal" by the standards of his day. In fact, in 1778 he drafted a bill for *proportioning* crimes and punishments in the Commonwealth of Virginia; that is, he wanted to see the punishment fit the crime and the criminal suffer no more than his offense deserved. Thus, a "member of society," as Jefferson phrased it,

> committing an inferior injury, does not wholly forfeit the protection of his fellow citizens, but after suffering a

punishment in proportion to his offense, is entitled to their protection from all greater pain . . .[1]

This was pretty progressive stuff back then, when just about anything that anybody did wrong was punishable by death. Jefferson felt that this was unfair and attempted to do something about it—but, insofar as the crime of murder was concerned, he was no abolitionist. He set up five categories of capital offenses:[2]

Treason. Death by hanging and forfeiture of all lands and goods to the Commonwealth.

Petty Treason (i.e., intrafamily killings). Death by hanging; ". . . his body [shall] be delivered up to the Anatomists to be dissected."

Murder by Poison. Death by poison.

Murder by way of a duel. Death by hanging and the body to be "gibbetted" (i.e., left on public display).

And finally:

Whoever shall commit murder in any other way shall suffer death by hanging.

That was the thinking of one of the more progressive of our forefathers, and that same thinking continues among the vast majority of our citizens to this very day, at least for the worst kinds of murder.

Historically there has always been a movement towards narrowing the classes of cases in which the death penalty could be invoked, and there is nothing wrong with that. Death is the supreme penalty and should only be meted out in those cases in which the crime was most heinous; the kinds of crimes that were described in the preceding chapter.

But the abolitionists were not satisfied with limiting the applicability of capital punishment; they wanted it thrown out altogether. They had their successes. By 1967, fourteen states had abolished or all but abolished the death penalty,[3] and nine more retained it for very limited categories of crimes.

These states had abolished capital punishment by legislation; however, by 1967 every other state had done so through

53

inertia. Although the death penalty was still on the books in most states, that year saw the last execution in this country for the next ten years.*

The abolitionists were riding higher than ever before.

One might have hoped that the blind faith the abolitionists had in the essential goodness of man, and their endless prattle about the sanctity of human life, would be vindicated. One might have hoped that the current crop of potential murderers would respond positively to the value that had been set on *their* lives by the abolitionist movement. Ideally, with all this talk of the "sanctity of life" and of "human dignity," the number of murders should have gone down.

However, criminals are a perverse and ungrateful lot, and they simply refused to justify the abolitionists' faith in their basic kindliness. In fact, some cynics began to believe that the criminals—murderers in particular—were actually doing the unthinkable and *taking advantage* of the efforts of the abolitionist movement to ensure that life would never again be taken for life. Cruel as it may sound, statistics seem to bear this out:

Year	Number of Executions	Number of Homicides
1955	76	7,000+
1960	56	8,000+
1966	1	10,000+
1972	0	18,000+
1975	0	20,000+

As we entered the early and mid-seventies, an interesting phenomenon occurred. The United States Supreme Court, in *Furman v. Georgia,* focused attention upon the capital punishment issue by outlawing it, while at the same time people were becoming more and more worried about their chances of being killed by some sort of criminal violence. With reason.

In 1975 Dr. Donald Lunde, a professor of law and psychiatry at Stanford University, produced a book called *Murder and Madness* that reported, not surprisingly, that we were "expe-

*Luis Jose Monge, 48, for murder, in Colorado on June 2, 1967. The method of execution was lethal gas.

riencing a murder epidemic that is breaking all previous records."[4]

In 1974 Dr. Arnold Barnett of the mathematics department of the Massachusetts Institute of Technology came up with the startling finding that a baby born in the United States in 1974 is more likely to be murdered than an American soldier in World War II was likely to be killed in combat. Dr. Barnett also predicted that if homicide rates continued to rise as they had in the past ten years, persons born in certain urban areas had the following statistical chances of being murdered:[5]

New York	1 in 17
Washington, D.C.	1 in 16
Chicago	1 in 24
Los Angeles	1 in 33
Atlanta	1 in 11
Miami	1 in 21
Detroit	1 in 14
Boston	1 in 32

Comparisons of homicides and battle deaths seem to be popular now, perhaps because they are something that people can relate to: the number of men killed in the worthy act of defending their country versus the number of innocent men and women whose lives have been senselessly wiped out by predators on the streets of America today. The FBI recently put historical perspective on such comparisons when it announced that annual murders in the United States were more than double U.S. battle deaths in the Revolutionary War (1775–1783), the War of 1812 (1812–1815), and the Mexican War (1846–1848).[6]

One scary aspect of the whole situation is that, at least in New York, the number of deliberate, stranger-to-stranger killings (as opposed to those in which the murderer is known to, or is even a member of the family of, the victim, and the killing is "spontaneous") is on the upsurge. According to a study published by the RAND Corporation in February of 1976, homicides in New York City soared from 968 per year in 1968 to 1,554 in 1974, a 60-percent increase. The study found that the major part of the city-wide rise in homicides seems to be in deliberate killings.[7]

This revelation, if it could be documented nationwide, would hit the abolitionist cause very hard. One of the movement's principal selling points has been the assertion that most murders are unpremeditated and spontaneous, arising from family quarrels; or are crimes of passion, committed by acquaintances who suddenly fall out. Thus the threat of death is unlikely to deter the killer.

"Look," the abolitionists said, "most murders are these little piddly intrafamily, Saturday-night-card-game, 'my-old-lady-was-stepping-out-on-me-so-I-shot-her' types of killings. We don't want to execute people just for *that*, do we?" The answer is "no, we don't." Even at common law, a killing in the heat of passion was held to be second-degree murder for which the death penalty was not exacted.

Okay, we concede that. Quick as a flash the crafty abolitionists moved into the breach. "Well, then," they said triumphantly, "since *most* killings are of the spontaneous kind, why should we set up a whole elaborate apparatus just to get at the Specks, Mansons, Lances, and Kelbachs? After all, those deliberate murders are sort of *de minimis*."

It might have worked, but as the RAND study indicates, those damnable Lances and Kelbachs, Gilmores, Dalton Williamses, and Freddie Martins were not about to leave well enough alone. They were going to continue to murder people, perfect strangers, in pretty terrifying ways, and the call for *their* execution grew louder as the depravity of their crimes increased.

Nevertheless, the state legislatures continued to recognize the difference between "spontaneous" crimes of passion and willful, brutal, premeditated murder. As was noted in Chapter 2, the Florida, Georgia, and Texas death penalty statutes that were upheld by the Supreme Court cover *only* the most hideous and aggravated sorts of crimes—primarily murder.

The clientele of the abolitionists is made up of all the actual and would-be murderers in the United States. It is an uncooperative sort of clientele; no sooner do the abolitionists get off something good about the sanctity of human life than some fool (no matter how sanctified his life) comes along and does such

56

a superterrible number on some innocent victims that it makes the "sanctity/human dignity" argument ring a bit hollow.

A case in point. Ira Schwartz, executive director of the John Howard Association, published a real bell-ringer called "The Crime of Capital Punishment" in the *Chicago Tribune* of December 5, 1976. In his article he gave us this little gem:

> Our society teaches us that human life is to be valued, that to kill is wrong, and yet society and the state sanction the crime of murder through the execution of those who violate our most revered laws.[8]

Lofty sentiments indeed. The reader is impressed.

Then along comes someone named Drabing, quoted in the same *Chicago Tribune* exactly ten days later, saying that after he murdered a Lincoln, Illinois farmer, Lloyd Schneider, his wife, and their 17-year-old daughter by inflicting on them 90 stab wounds in all, he felt excited and planned to kill more people.[9]

Thanks a *lot*, Mike Drabing! We just get rolling on the value of human life and then you come along with the "I liked the blood" bit. That will be really helpful when they consider the death penalty down in Springfield.

Intransigent as their clientele may be, the abolitionists plan to keep at it. A moth doesn't know any better than to charge that light bulb until he is burned up and falls, pathetically, to the ground. The light bulb may be public opinion and the moth the abolitionists. Kindness *must* win out, they assert, but Mike Drabing tied up Terri Schneider, turned off the lights, and played a Beatles record as he waited for her parents to come home. She knew what was in store for her as she lay there terrified. That sort of thing tends to sour the milk of human kindness.

What about public opinion and the death penalty?

We can assume that most people, particularly in the inner cities, where the threat of day-to-day violence is as constant a factor as, say, going to work or the noncollection of garbage, have not read Dr. Lunde's study of murder, or the MIT study of murder risk vs. World War II combat deaths, or the RAND

57

study of deliberate homicides in New York (worthy as all three studies may be).

Why, then, do we hear such a clamor for a return to capital punishment? The answer is that the average citizen doesn't need any studies to tell him that he's scared.

The threat of street crime is sufficient to keep a sizable number of our citizens in fear: in their neighborhoods and even inside their own homes. In July 1975 the Gallup Poll reported that 45 percent of the citizens of the United States were afraid to walk the streets of their neighborhoods at night. The figure was up from 31 percent in 1968. Significantly, the number of those afraid to go out at night rose to 57 percent among non-whites, proving (if proof were needed) that crime bears down hardest on the poor and powerless and those who live in our urban ghettoes. That same Gallup Poll revealed that 19 percent of all surveyed, and 33 percent of nonwhites, were fearful at night *even while in their own homes.*[10]

So, he is afraid, that average citizen. What is he *most* afraid of? The natural instinct for self-preservation being what it is, a good guess would be that his principal fear is that he might be killed.

Maybe that is why we are getting these numbers from the pollsters about capital punishment. The Gallup and Harris polls, almost uncannily accurate barometers of public opinion, have in recent years charted a steady rise in public support for capital punishment:[11]

GALLUP	Favor Capital Punishment	Oppose Capital Punishment	Not Sure or No Opinion
1976	65	28	7
1972	57	32	11
1971	49	40	11
1966	42	47	11
HARRIS			
1977	67	25	8
1973	59	31	10
1970	47	42	11
1969	48	38	14

In addition to the public opinion polls, when we consider the results of capital punishment referenda in three states, we find support for the contention that most people believe death is a proper penalty for certain of the more heinous crimes.

Illinois put the question on the ballot in 1970 and 1,217,791 voted to retain against 676,302 for abolishment, a margin of almost two to one.[12] The California Supreme Court, as noted above, ruled in 1972 that capital punishment violated the *California* constitution.[13] Citizens of the Golden State, resenting the fact that six unelected justices had appointed themselves as a sort of superlegislature, obtained with ease the required number of signatures to place on the November ballot Proposition 17, a measure to reinstate capital punishment in the California constitution.

Proposition 17 passed by a two-to-one margin.[14] The vote was taken a scant four months after four-year-old Joyce Ann Huff had been deliberately shotgunned to death while playing in her yard the previous July. We will never be able to prove it, but quite possibly a number of the lopsided majority of voters for reinstatement remembered this particularly revolting crime. Newspaper accounts of the killing had encouraged the "appeal to the raw emotions" that was decried by Dean E. Donald Shapiro in the previous chapter. ("Tot, Playing in Yard, Dies" might be an example of a newspaper headline that did *not* appeal to the emotions.) We can wish with all our hearts that Joyce Ann had not been killed, but perhaps her death, and the manner in which she died, convinced some of the undecided voters that, yes, we must henceforth put a premium on little lives like hers and execute the people who commit such murders.

Two-to-one seems to be the going rate for retention or restoration of the death penalty. In 1975 the voters of the State of Washington approved capital punishment by that margin.[15]

None of these expressions of public support for capital punishment can have been good news for the committed abolitionists. It is all very well for them to know in their own hearts that they are right—and, perhaps to their credit, they never waver in that conviction—but they have to face facts. Roughly 65 percent of the general population doesn't agree with them; and, at least according to Gallup, that 65 percent is up from 42 percent only ten years before, a jump of 23 percentage points. Which is pretty sizable any way you look at it.

And finally, of course, the capstone to the entire public opinion contention is to be found in the fact that 35 state legislatures and the federal government, which we can assume reflect the will of the majority of their constituents, reinstated the death penalty after *Furman*, at least for some crimes.

Why? What has caused such a hardening of opinion in this supposedly enlightened society? Well, the word "enlightened" can mean different things to different people. To some it suggests an automatic favorable response to all things liberal, kindly, noble, compassionate, and so on. But it can also mean that people are simply getting smart.

One aspect of being smart is the ability to make the connection between cause and effect, and so we find a correlation between the increasing murder toll and increasing support for the death penalty in the United States:

1966 — 10,920 murders
         42 percent support capital punishment, 47 percent
         oppose

1975 — 20,510 murders
         65 percent support captial punishment, 28 percent
         oppose

(Gallup)

Any good abolitionist statistician could probably devise a number of ways to make mincemeat of the contention that there is a correlation between increased support for the death penalty and a doubling in the number of homicides in ten years; but on a commonsense basis it's worth considering.

We may get an inkling of why so many people have switched on the capital punishment issue by listening to some thoughtful writers who have changed or modified their positions.

Jim Bishop, columnist and author (*The Day Kennedy Was Shot, The Day Christ Died*), tells us in a piece written in April 1976 that he has been opposed to capital punishment for years:

> And yet, I waver in my belief. Crime in our streets is out
> of control. Our prisons are jammed. Criminals out on bail
> for one violent crime commit another. Some filling stations
> and bars sustain three and four holdups each year.

Nowhere in the article does Bishop actually state that he has become a proponent of the death penalty, but he does say:

> If my opposition to capital punishment must melt against
> the heat of public opinion—so be it. But go all the way.[16]

He then comes up with some pretty hard-line stuff about mandatory life sentences for three-time recidivists and abolishing parole boards. It sort of buttresses the thesis that as violent crime increases, apparently unchecked, the public response will get tougher and tougher.

One philosopher who did a 180-degree turn is Professor Burton M. Leiser, chairman of the philosophy department at Drake University. Let the abolitionists ponder his words if they wonder why 23 percent of our population departed the abolitionist camp in the past ten years:

> Because human life is sacred, the death penalty should
> be restored with all deliberate speed.
> As a former advocate of abolition of capital punishment,
> I write these words with deep regret, for the humanitarian
> motives of those who oppose the deliberate execution of
> any man must find a sympathetic echo in the heart of every
> person who has an ounce of compassion within him. However, those very humanitarian objectives inevitably lead to
> the conclusion that some persons must be put to death.
> And anyone who is seized with a sense of compassion for
> suffering humanity and is not committed to a doctrinaire
> refusal to allow the taking of human life under any circumstances ought, in my opinion, to agree that the death penalty is an evil that cannot be avoided so long as some men
> continue to disregard the vital interests of their fellow
> men.[17]

There we have it. Spoken by a philosopher. The man in the street might put it differently, but the sentiment, whether expressed thoughtfully or crudely, is the same: the penalty for murder-most-foul should be death.

61

The abolitionists call the execution of a human being "barbarous." The Supreme Court of the United States does not call it barbarous. It would be "cruel and unusual" punishment if it were barbarous, and that is prohibited by the Eighth Amendment to the United States Constitution. The Court held in 1890 in the *Kemmler*[18] case that:

> Punishments are cruel when they involve torture or lingering death; but the punishment of death is not cruel, within the meaning of that word as used in the Constitution. It implies something inhuman and barbarous, something more than the mere extinguishment of life.

Nor has the Court ever deviated from this position.

So judicial execution is lawful under the Constitution of the United States. But it can't be a very pleasant thing for anybody involved. Certainly not for the condemned, for the corrections officials, or (with the exception of a lunatic fringe who *want* to watch an execution and for that reason alone should be excluded) for the witnesses.

It is no frivolous thing to take someone from a holding cell, march him into an execution chamber, and hang, gas, electrocute, or shoot him. That's how we do it in this country and it can't be pleasant.

Let's take the description of one double execution: the hangings of Richard Eugene Hickock and Perry Edward Smith, April 14, 1965, for the murders of Mr. and Mrs. Herbert Clutter and their two children, Kenyon and Nancy, in November 1959 at their farm house in Holcomb, Kansas.

This was the case that Truman Capote made famous in his masterful "nonfiction novel" *In Cold Blood.** It tells of the crime, the flight, the capture, the trial, and, finally, the execution; it is probably the best thing of its kind ever written. Mr. Capote, in writing *In Cold Blood*, got to know Smith and Hickock well; he attended their execution. If we must deal with the realities of judicial execution, there is no more graphic and sensitive a portrayal.**

*New York: Random House (1965).

**If the reader is interested in further graphic, if somewhat sensational, descriptions of executions, complete with pictures, I refer him to an article by Keith R. Benet entitled "The Return of the Death Penalty" in *True Magazine*, May 1975, p. 23.

Dewey [the Kansas Bureau of Investigation agent most responsible for their capture] had watched them die, for he had been among the twenty-odd witnesses invited to the ceremony. He had never attended an execution, and when on the midnight past he entered the cold warehouse, the scenery had surprised him: he had anticipated a setting of suitable dignity, not this bleakly lighted cavern cluttered with lumber and other debris. But the gallows itself, with its two pale nooses attached to a crossbeam, was imposing enough; and so, in an unexpected style, was the hangman, who cast a long shadow from his perch on the platform at the top of the wooden instrument's thirteen steps. The hangman, an anonymous, leathery gentleman who had been imported from Missouri for the event, for which he was paid six hundred dollars, was attired in an aged double-breasted pin-striped suit overly commodious for the narrow figure inside it—the coat came nearly to his knees; and on his head he wore a cowboy hat which, when first bought, had perhaps been bright green, but was now a weathered, sweat-stained oddity.

Also, Dewey found the self-consciously casual conversation of his fellow witnesses, as they stood awaiting the start of what one witness termed "the festivities," disconcerting.

"What I heard was, they was gonna let them draw straws to see who dropped first. Or flip a coin. But Smith says why not do it alphabetically. Guess 'cause S comes after H. Ha!"

"Read in the paper, afternoon paper, what they ordered for their last meal? Ordered the same menu. Shrimp. French fries. Garlic bread. Ice cream and strawberries and whipped cream. Understand Smith didn't touch his much."

"That Hickock's got a sense of humor. They was telling me how, about an hour ago, one of the guards says to him, 'This must be the longest night of your life.' And Hickock, he laughs and says, 'No. The shortest.' "

"Did you hear about Hickock's eyes? He left them to an eye doctor. Soon as they cut him down, this doctor's gonna yank out his eyes and stick them in somebody else's head. Can't say I'd want to be that somebody. I'd feel peculiar with them eyes in my head."

"Christ! Is that *rain*? All the windows down! My new Chevy. Christ!"

The sudden rain rapped the high warehouse roof. The sound, not unlike the rat-a-tat-tat of parade drums, heralded Hickock's arrival. Accompanied by six guards and a prayer-murmuring chaplain, he entered the death place handcuffed and wearing an ugly harness of leather straps that bound his arms to his torso. At the foot of the gallows the warden read to him the official order of execution, a two-page document; and as the warden read, Hickock's eyes, enfeebled by half a decade of cell shadows, roamed the little audience until, not seeing what he sought, he asked the nearest guard, in a whisper, if any member of the Clutter family was present. When he was told no, the prisoner seemed disappointed, as though he thought the protocol surrounding this ritual of vengeance was not being properly observed.

As is customary, the warden, having finished his recitation, asked the condemned man whether he had any last statement to make. Hickock nodded. "I just want to say I hold no hard feelings. You people are sending me to a better world than this ever was"; then, as if to emphasize the point, he shook hands with the four men mainly responsible for his capture and conviction, all of whom had requested permission to attend the executions: F.B.I. Agents Roy Church, Clarence Duntz, Harold Nye, and Dewey himself. "Nice to see you," Hickock said with his most charming smile; it was as if he were greeting guests at his own funeral.

The hangman coughed—impatiently lifted his cowboy hat and settled it again, a gesture somehow reminiscent of a turkey buzzard huffing, then smoothing its neck feathers —and Hickock, nudged by an attendant, mounted the scaffold steps. "The Lord giveth, the Lord taketh away. Blessed is the name of the Lord," the chaplain intoned, as the rain sound accelerated, as the noose was fitted, and as a delicate black mask was tied round the prisoner's eyes. "May the Lord have mercy on your soul." The trap door opened, and Hickock hung for all to see a full twenty minutes before the prison doctor at last said, "I pronounce this man dead." A hearse, its blazing headlights beaded with rain, drove into the warehouse, and the body, placed on a litter and shrouded under a blanket, was carried to the hearse and out into the night.

Staring after it, Roy Church shook his head: "I never would have believed he had the guts. To take it like he did. I had him tagged a coward."

The man to whom he spoke, another detective, said, "Aw, Roy. The guy was a punk. A mean bastard. He deserved it."

Church, with thoughtful eyes, continued to shake his head.

While waiting for the second execution, a reporter and a guard conversed. The reporter said, "This your first hanging?"

"I seen Lee Andrews."

"This here's my first."

"Yeah. How'd you like it?"

The reporter pursed his lips. "Nobody in our office wanted the assignment. Me either. But it wasn't as bad as I thought it would be. Just like jumping off a diving board. Only with a rope around your neck."

"They don't feel nothing. Drop, snap, and that's it. They don't feel nothing."

"Are you sure? I was standing right close, I could hear him gasping for breath."

"Uh-huh, but he don't feel nothing. Wouldn't be humane if he did."

"Well. And I suppose they feed them a lot of pills. Sedatives."

"Hell, no. Against the rules. Here comes Smith."

"Gosh, I didn't know he was such a shrimp."

"Yeah, he's little. But so is a tarantula."

As he was brought into the warehouse, Smith recognized his old foe, Dewey; he stopped chewing a hunk of Doublemint gum he had in his mouth, and grinned and winked at Dewey, jaunty and mischievous. But after the warden asked if he had anything to say, his expression was sober. His sensitive eyes gazed gravely at the surrounding faces, swerved up to the shadowy hangman, then downward to his own manacled hands. He looked at his fingers, which were stained with ink and paint, for he'd spent his final three years on Death Row painting self-portraits and pictures of children, usually the children of inmates who supplied him with photographs of their seldom-seen progeny. "I think," he said, "it's a helluva thing to take a life in this manner. I don't believe in capital punishment, morally or legally. Maybe I had something to contribute, something—" His assurance faltered, shyness blurred his voice, lowered it to a just audible level. "It would be meaningless to apologize for what I did. Even inappropriate. But I do. I apologize."

Steps, noose, mask; but before the mask was adjusted, the prisoner spat his chewing gum into the chaplain's outstretched palm. Dewey shut his eyes; he kept them shut until he heard the thud-snap that announces a rope-broken neck. Like the majority of American law-enforcement officials, Dewey is certain that capital punishment is a deterrent to violent crime, and he felt that if ever the penalty had been earned, the present instance was it. The preceding execution had not disturbed him, he had never had much use for Hickock, who seemed to him "a small-time chiseler who got out of his depth, empty and worthless."

65

But Smith, though he was the true murderer, aroused another response, for Perry possessed a quality, the aura of an exiled animal, a creature walking wounded, that the detective could not disregard. He remembered his first meeting with Perry in the interrogation room at Police Headquarters in Las Vegas—the dwarfish boy-man seated in the metal chair, his small booted feet not quite brushing the floor. And when Dewey now opened his eyes, that is what he saw: the same childish feet, tilted, dangling.

That is what happens. The story may vary with the method of execution but the script is the same. A man (or woman) is led forcibly to death.

We have tried to make the act itself as humane as possible. That is, we have cut to a minimum the actual time it takes the condemned man to die. Any method of execution must, of necessity, cause physical pain, but we try to keep it fleeting.

Hanging is, by all reports, the fastest—if the hangman knows his business. The neck snaps and the condemned man knows nothing else.* Unfortunately, many hangmen did not know what they were about and a number of botched hangings in New York in the 1880s led to a search for a better, quicker means of execution. Theodore Bernstein, a professor of electrical engineering, describes the quest:

> They thought of shooting, the garrote, the guillotine and other things but they were all too messy. They thought of lethal injections, but no doctors would do it.[19]

Electricity was becoming popular, and since people who were accidentally electrocuted didn't seem to suffer much, this method of dispatch was looked into.

> There was a big political thing over how legal electrocutions should be done between Thomas Edison and George Westinghouse.
> Edison was against capital punishment but said if it was done it should be done with Westinghouse's alternating current because it was more dangerous.
> There was no word for electrocution at the time and Edison wanted it to be called Westinghousing.[20]

*For a fascinating, unsensationalized account of the technique of judicial hanging, see *Executioner: Pierrepoint*, London: Coronet Books (1974), the autobiography of one of England's chief hangmen.

This bickering was eventually resolved, and one William Kemmler became the first person to be executed by electrocution on August 6, 1890.

By 1959 electrocution was pretty fast. Charles Starkweather walked into the death chamber of the Nebraska State penitentiary at 12:01 A.M. of June 25. He was strapped in the electric chair, the current was turned on and he was pronounced dead at 12:04. Elapsed time: three minutes.[21]

Nevada introduced lethal gas in 1924, and one Gee Jon was the first man to be executed this way. A newspaper editorial commented:

> It brings us one step further from the savage state where we seek vengence and retaliatory pain infliction.[22]

By 1972, nineteen states electrocuted their condemned men, eight used lethal gas, and seven used hanging.[23]

It is ironic that the first man in ten years to die by execution of judicial sentence, Gary Mark Gilmore, met his reward in the one state that retains the firing squad as a means of execution. (Utah gives the condemned man a choice between hanging and shooting.) Shooting could result in almost instantaneous death if the hands of the squad members are steady, and they were for Gilmore. Two minutes after the bullets of the four marksmen who used live ammunition thudded into his heart, all of his vital signs were extinguished.

There is a certain machismo about facing the firing squad, though, and that was quite obviously a factor in Gilmore's death wish. The procedure in Utah is to strap the condemned man into a chair with a hood over his head and a target over his heart. Gilmore wanted to stand, with no blindfold, facing the firing squad, but he didn't get his wish in this regard.

And that seems to be all that we can do to make the process as swift and painless as possible. The state of California, in 1973, set up a special commission to study alternative methods of execution. Like their colleagues in New York in the 1880s, the panel looked around and came to the same conclusion. There were no acceptable methods that offered an advantage over the time-tested ways to execute people.[24]

We seem to be stuck with the conventional methods of execution. They are certainly fast enough, but that doesn't detract much from the grisly ritual of the whole thing: the set date, the waiting, the death watch; finally, "Come along, Joe. It's time." But it isn't barbarous and it *is* necessary.

To sum up. The penalty for murder in the United States was death at the time of Thomas Jefferson. The penalty for murder in the United States is death now. But only for those most horrible cases that the legislatures, in their wisdom, have chosen to classify as capital murder.

Notes

1. Thomas Jefferson, "A Bill for Proportioning Crimes and Punishments, in cases heretofore Capital," *The Writings of Thomas Jefferson*, issued under the auspices of the Thomas Jefferson Memorial Association of the United States, Washington, D.C.(1905), vol. 1, p. 218.
2. *Ibid.*, p. 221 ff.
3. Federal Bureau of Prisons, U.S. Department of Justice, *Uniform Crime Reports, 1967* (Washington, D.C., 1968), pp.62–79.
4. Donald Lunde, "Murder and Madness," Stanford Alumni Association, Bowman Alumni House, Stanford, Calif. 94305, as noted in *Parade* magazine, August 17, 1975.
5. "Murder Study Says Life More Hazardous Than WWII Combat," *Crime Control Digest*, April 15, 1974, p. 3, col. 2.
6. FBI Law Enforcement Bulletin, April 1976, p. 3, col. 2.
7. Selwin Raab, " 'Deliberate' Slayings on Increase Here," *New York Times*, February 27, 1976, p. 1, col. 6.
8. Ira Schwartz, "The Crime of Capital Punishment," *Chicago Tribune*, Dec. 5, 1976, sec. 2, p. 1, col. 4.
9. Ronald Koziol, " 'I Liked the Blood'—Accused Killer," *Chicago Tribune*, December 15, 1976, sec. 1, p. 6, col. 1.
10. George Gallup, "45% Afraid to Go Out at Night," *Chicago Sun-Times*, July 28, 1975, p. 1, col. 1.
11. These figures are taken from various newspaper accounts describing the results of the polls: "57% in Poll Back Death Penalty," *New York Times*, Nov. 22, 1972, p. 18c, col. 4. Louis Harris, "New Favor for Death Penalty," *Chicago Tribune*, June 11, 1973, sec. 1, p. 26, col. 6. Jerrold K. Footlick and Lucy Howard, "Dusting Off 'Old Sparky,' " *Newsweek*, November 29, 1976, p. 35, col. 1. "A Majority Now Favors Executions," *Chicago Tribune*, February 7, 1977, sec. 4, p. 4, col. 6.
12. Illinois Secretary of State, Constitution of the State of Illinois and the United States, pp. 13, 15 (1971).

13. *People v. Anderson,* Cal. Sup. Ct., 493 P. 2d 880 (1972).
14. See *CLO News,* a publication of Citizens for Law and Order, P.O. Box 13131, Oakland, Calif. 94661, no. 40, March, 1974, p. 1, col. 1.
15. *Criminal Law Reporter,* November 26, 1975, vol. 18, p. 2196, col. 2.
16. Jim Bishop, "Death Penalty and the Nation's Highest Court," *Los Angeles Herald-Examiner,* April 17, 1976, p. A-12, col. 2.
17. Burton Leiser, "In Defense of Capital Punishment," *The Barrister,* Fall 1974, p. 10.
18. 136 U.S. 436 (1890).
19. "Electric Chair, Its Origins, History and Use as Explained by Professor," *Crime Control Digest,* November 1, 1976, p. 4, col. 1.
20. *Ibid.*
21. William Allen, *Starkweather: The Story of a Mass Murderer,* Boston: Houghton Mifflin (1976), p. 175 ff.
22. Hugo Bedau, *The Death Penalty in America,* New York: Doubleday (1967), reprinted in McCafferty, ed., *Capital Punishment,* Chicago: Aldine-Atherton Co. (1972), p. 22.
23. "Controversy Over Capital Punishment," *Congressional Digest,* January 1973, p. 5, col. 2.
24. "California Study Results in Decision to Retain Use of Gas Chamber," *Criminal Justice Digest,* November 1973, p. 8, col. 1.

Part II

THE ARGUMENTS

CHAPTER 4

Criminals' Rights vs. Victims' Rights

In terms of decor and sheer grandeur, it must be one of the most imposing chambers in the world. The tall white columns, the red curtain, and so on.

In terms of pure raw power, it must be *the* most imposing chamber in the world: the courtroom of the Supreme Court of the United States.

There they sit, the nine men who had the power to wipe out a presidency, who could strike the entire legislative efforts of Congress and all of the fifty states off the books if they were so minded. They took this power upon themselves in 1803 when Chief Justice John Marshall wrote the Court's opinion in *Marbury v. Madison*.[1] The Supreme Court, said the Supreme Court, is the final arbiter of the Constitution of the United States: legislators can legislate, executives can execute, but if we decide that an issue has Constitutional dimensions, what we say goes.

Someone has to come out on top. The framers of the Constitution envisaged three coequal branches of government and this they tried hard to ensure. But the laws of governmental inertia virtually guaranteed that someone would turn up more equal than the others, and that someone was the Supreme Court.

The Court had proved that it was more equal when, in 1972, it overturned the death penalty laws of the United States government and 40 states. Now, in 1976, five of the states were back again with death penalty statutes that, they hoped, conformed with the Court's prior pronouncements. Would there be another wipeout?

Anthony Amsterdam* is one of the best criminal-law appellate attorneys in the country, perhaps in the world. To paraphrase Voltaire: "I disagree with what he says, but I sure as hell admire the skill with which he says it."

He was asking the Court for another wipeout—a repeat performance of 1972: he wanted the justices to overturn the death penalty statutes of the 35 states that had reenacted capital punishment laws in the wake of the *Furman* decision. If anyone could convince the Court, it would be Tony Amsterdam.

Harry Blackmun is far and away the kindliest-looking justice on the Supreme Court. He is a thoughtful but not a doctrinaire conservative. He is his own man, which he proved when he wrote what is perhaps his most famous opinion: *Roe v. Wade*,[2] the decision that held that states could not constitutionally prohibit abortions in most instances, a decision that pleased the majority of liberals and drove a lot of conservatives up the wall.

Justice Blackmun is a compassionate man, too. He dissented, when the five-justice majority in the *Furman* case declared that capital punishment as then applied was unconstitutional, on the grounds that the High Court had no business swinging a meat axe at the good-faith efforts of state legislators to protect their citizens. But he went on record as a personal foe of capital punishment:

> I yield to no one in the depth of my distaste, antipathy and indeed abhorrence for the death penalty. . . .[3]

Now, in 1976, the issue was back before the Court and some of the abolitionists—naively—hoped that Mr. Justice Blackmun

*Professor of Law, Stanford University

had changed his position since *Furman* and would vote with their cause. He didn't. In fact, he indicated that his compassion lay in more than one direction.

He threw a zinger at Professor Amsterdam:

> If you wanted to argue for retribution for murder, the victims—*whom you have never mentioned*—have already lost.[4] [emphasis supplied]

Uh, oh! Why did he have to say *that? Of course* Tony Amsterdam hadn't said anything about the victims of murder; he is a brilliant advocate and he was not about to throw away his case by bringing up the fatal weakness in it.

But there it was. Justice Blackmun, in his quiet way, had reminded counsel that the victims of crime just might be entitled to some consideration by the Court.

Justice Byron R. White, who, paradoxically, had voted with the majority in *Furman* (but who also voted with the majority in *Gregg, Jurek,* and *Proffitt* to restore capital punishment), had raised the matter of victims some six years earlier.

White wrote a blistering dissent in the 1966 case of *Miranda v. Arizona*,[5] in which the Court, in a 5–4 opinion, held that confessions by criminal suspects could not be used against them unless preceded by a litany of warnings to the suspect about his rights. Joined by Justice Potter Stewart and the late Justice John Marshall Harlan, Jr., Justice White grimly pointed out that any number of guilty people would now have to be released to continue their criminal endeavors. He then said with supreme irony:

> There is, of course, a saving factor: the next victims are un-*certain, unnamed, and unrepresented* in this case.[6] [emphasis supplied]

So attention *is* paid to the plight of the victims at the highest judicial level in the nation. Justice Blackmun's little shot would not do the abolitionist cause much good. But it hit the nail on the head. When we discuss the controversial and emotional issue of capital punishment, the two sides are divided, never to meet, by the stark question: *Who are you for, the criminal or the victim?*

Now, I anticipate some reaction to that last statement. The

abolitionists, who I readily concede are men of compassion and good will, will say that they are *not* against the victim; that, indeed, they feel very sorry for the victim; they may go so far as to deplore the horror and suffering inflicted upon the victim by the murderer. They just don't want the murderer executed for it.

Utter nonsense. You cannot have it both ways. If you go to bat for the "sanctity" of the life of the murderer, you are by definition taking a stance completely opposed to his victim or victims.

First, on a rather theoretical level, when the abolitionists fight so tirelessly (and successfully) to spare the life of, say, Richard Speck, they are at the same time saying that the lives of Gloria Davy, Suzanne Farris, Merlita Gargullo, Mary Ann Jordan, Patricia Matusek, Valentina Pasion, Nina Jo Schmale, and Pamela Wilkening are of little consequence. Our criminal-justice system (which did nothing whatsoever to protect them) must consign them to obscurity and bend all of its efforts to keep the man who killed them happily watching television in the penitentiary and hoping for parole.

The contention that because human life is sacred, we should not execute any murderers, no matter how vile, mocks the sanctity of the lives of the victims. Were the lives of those eight student nurses worth nothing more than an easy jail term, perhaps someday shortened by parole, for Richard Speck? Is society forbidden to express outrage at the crime by executing the murderer?

On a far more practical level, we have the question of deterrence of future murderers, which will be discussed in detail in a subsequent chapter. Here we are considering only the antivictim attitude of the abolitionists. They say that the death penalty does not deter murderers. Why? "Well, we have some studies and—well, we just don't believe that it does."

There is a lot of evidence that capital punishment *would* deter murderers if it were enforced. Apparently an awful lot of people—the two-to-one ratio of public support for the death penalty, for example—believe it is a deterrent. And certainly the fact that the number of homicides in this country doubled from about 10,000 to 20,000 annually during the ten-year period in which capital punishment was, for all intents and purposes, defunct indicates that anything *less* than that sanction is no deterrent at all. To withhold the threat of death may even *encourage* murders.

But, assuming for the sake of argument that the proponents cannot prove, with mathematical certainty, that capital punishment deters, the abolitionists can no more prove that it does not (except to themselves). So whose side do they line up on? The convicted criminals', of course. If they are wrong—if as some studies show, each execution would deter several murders, or even one—then thousands of innocent victims could have been spared.

If capital punishment does *not* deter others, the worst we have done is to execute convicted murderers. If it *does* deter, we have virtually ensured that without it more people will be murdered. Whom do we take a chance with, the killers or their potential victims? Why, the killers of course, say the abolitionists; *we* can't be concerned about the victims. They're already dead, remember?

Then we have those cases in which someone murders his victim; he is convicted; but his life is spared and then he escapes from prison or is released from prison and kills someone else; or he kills someone while in prison. Such cases do happen, as we will see. Now we have some *actual* victims (as opposed to potential victims in the deterrence/nondeterrence argument) for the abolitionists. They reply that human life is sacred . . .

These are the reasons why I accuse the abolitionist forces of being antivictim. But don't take my word for it. Let one of them tell you himself. Alan Goldstein, a legal staffer for the Maryland affiliate of the American Civil Liberties Union, which has been preeminent in the abolitionist movement, was interviewed by Barbara Palmer of the *Washington Star-News:*

> QUESTION: You have been outspoken in your opposition to the movement to strengthen the rights of victims. You have stated that "victims don't have rights." Could you explain this?
>
> GOLDSTEIN: Well, I don't mean that victims don't have rights in a general sense. But what they really are in the criminal-justice process, are witnesses for the prosecution, and in that sense they do not have constitutional rights which are guaranteed to the defendant.[7]

Tell *that* to the wives of Max Jensen and Bennie Bushnell who were executed by Gary Mark Gilmore. Or, for that matter, tell it to Thomas Jefferson; that his Bill of Rights has become so perverted in some minds that it is now a document designed solely for the protection of the criminal defendant.

The ACLU attorneys launched an energetic and totally unwanted campaign to spare Gary Gilmore's life. They were, they said, protecting his "rights"; despite the fact that he railed at them and told them to "butt out." Naturally they were blithely unconcerned for any rights his victims might have had, and in view of the statement of their colleague Mr. Goldstein from the other end of the continent, I suppose they were at least consistent.

It is pretty obvious that the abolitionists do not want to hear anything about the victims; recall Justice Blackmun's pointed comment to Professor Amsterdam about the victims " . . . whom you have never mentioned . . ." But those pesky victims just won't seem to go away. The common man is too mule-headed, too intransigent to concede that the death penalty should be debated in a sort of sterilized clinical arena, with no reference to the injuries, indignities, and cruelties inflicted upon the victims by the people who murdered them.

In a vacuum Charles Manson is an interesting social and psychological phenomenon; but when we see the picture of Mr. La Bianca's murdered body, with the carving fork sticking out of it, Charles Manson becomes a monster.

During the explosion of death penalty legislation after *Furman*, the abolitionists, seeing the handwriting on the wall, sometimes introduced foolish amendments to such legislation in order to point up the "grotesqueness" of the penalty. Harassing tactics. One such amendment would have required that executions be televised on prime time.[8]

No such legislation has ever been passed, nor is it likely to be; but let us speculate for a moment. Suppose that it *was* passed and that the decision on what to air was left solely to a proponent and an opponent of the death penalty. They meet.

The abolitionist says: "I want the execution of so-and-so televised on prime time because, to be perfectly honest with you, I believe that the airing of this grisly spectacle will set in motion such a wave of revulsion against 'legalized murder' that there will be an immediate and emphatic groundswell against capital punishment.''

"Fine," says the proponent. "I'm with you all the way. But, I have a little something that I'm going to throw in, too. Before we terrorize all of those good people with pictures of an execution, I want to show them the crime-scene photographs of the bodies of the victims *and* the autopsy photographs; then Detective Adams here, who worked on the case, will tell them about what he saw at the crime scene; then the coroner will describe *his* findings. Then, and only then, will the cameras pan in on the poor wretch in the execution chamber.''

"You can't do that," says the abolitionist, livid with rage. "You would be appealing to 'raw emotions'!''

"And you're not?" the proponent replies. "After all, reality is reality. Of course, if you wish to cancel the whole thing . . .''

This may sound a little farfetched; but is it really? The abolitionists will do everything in their power to picture the condemned as a victim; and they are completely sincere—that is how they picture him. But they don't want you to get started about the victim of the crime itself. What does *that* have to do with it?

Guilt, like beauty, lies in the eye of the beholder. If you hammer at the issue of the victims of crime, and if you call for the punishment of those who are guilty, then by some Alice in Wonderland sort of logic, the guilt shifts to you.

That is the thesis of Dr. Karl Menninger, who tells us:

> I suspect that all the crimes committed by all the jailed criminals does not equal in total social damages all of the crimes committed against them.[9]

Now this is bad enough if you happen to be victim-oriented and believe that a murderer *should* be punished, but then Dr. Menninger hits us with the follow-up: we are guilty for even *calling* criminals "criminals." He tells us:

> And there is one crime we all keep committing, over and over. I accuse the reader of this—and myself too—and all the non-readers. We commit the crime of damning some of our fellow citizens with the label "criminal." And having done this, we force them through an experience that is soul-searing and dehumanizing.[10]

All right. I plead guilty to the violation of such enlightened principles. I call murderers "criminals" and I advocate that they be punished.

But I don't feel guilty. Somehow or other I can't seem to get bent out of shape by using the word "criminal" to describe Richard Speck, Charles Manson, Lance and Kelbach, or Gary Mark Gilmore. Nor for stating that they should have been, or should now be, executed. And I can't help feeling that the families of their victims might agree with me.

New York State Supreme Court Justice Joseph A. Martinis sentenced one Hosie S. Turner to 25 years to life in prison for murdering a 28-year-old woman while robbing her of $7. The defendant had 16 prior convictions for robbery, burglary, larceny, possession and sale of drugs, and parole violations. Justice Martinis told him he would have sentenced him to death if the law permitted, adding:

> Lost in the maze of protective steps for the accused are the civil and constitutional rights of the victims, and those left behind when the victim is killed.[11]

We have then a real cleavage between the attitude of the abolitionists and that of the proponents of capital punishment. The split is over concern for the victim. Dr. Sidney Hook, professor of philosophy at Stanford University and one of the world's leading civil libertarians—but a tough-minded one—sums up the situation. Noting first that any citizen might be wrongly accused of a crime, he weighed the risks in the balance:

> Granted that I am a potential criminal. I am also a potential victim of crime. The U.S. statistics of mounting violence show that cases of murder, non-negligent manslaughter and forcible rape have skyrocketed. It has been estimated that in America's large metropolitan centers, the risk of becoming a victim of crime has doubled in the last decade. Since many crimes of violence are committed by repeaters, the likelihood of my becoming a victim of crime is much greater than the likelihood of my becoming a criminal. Therefore, the protection of my rights not to be mugged, assaulted, or murdered looms much larger in my mind than my rights as a criminal defendant.
>
> Let us be clear about some things that have become obscured by our legitimate concern with the rights of crimi-

nals and those accused of crime. The potential victim has at least just as much a human right not to be violently molested, interfered with, and outraged as the person accused of such crimes has to a fair trial and a skillful defense. As a citizen most of the rights guaranteed me under the Bill of Rights become nugatory if I am hopelessly crippled and all of them become extinguished if I am killed.[12]

Precisely. And that is why the victims must be given a voice in the debate over capital punishment. The next victim could be you or me.

Notes

1. 1 Cranch (U.S.) 137, 2 L. Ed. 60 (1803).
2. 410 U.S. 113 (1973).
3. 408 U.S. 238, p. 405.
4. David Breasted, "U.S. Backs States on Death Penalty," *Pittsburgh Press*, April 1, 1976, p. 6. col. 1.
5. 384 U.S. 436 (1966).
6. *Ibid.*, p. 543.
7. Barbara Palmer, "The Rights of Victims: A Differing View," *Washington Star-News*, July 8, 1975, p. 1, col. 1.
8. "Capital Punishment, 1973: Just as Cruel and More Unusual Every Day," a staff report, *Juris Doctor*, December 1973, p. 12, col. 1.
9. Karl Menninger, *The Crime of Punishment*, New York: Viking Press (1969), p. 17.
10. *Ibid.*, p. 9.
11. Marcia Chambers, "Justice, Sentencing Killer, Urges Death Penalty Law," *New York Times*, February 8, 1975, p. 29C, col. 7.
12. Sidney Hook, "The Rights of Victims: A Reflection on Crime and Compassion," *Encounter*, March 1972.

CHAPTER 5

Death and Deterrence

The question whether future murders will de deterred by the statutory availability *and the application* of the death penalty is far and away the most important argument in the entire controversy. No airtight mathematical proof for or against the deterrent value of capital punishment is available to us now, although scientists on either side of the question have come up with their own analyses and a lively, if rather arcane, debate is raging today.

The basic reason for the lack of certainty in the statistical battle is obvious: it is very difficult to prove a negative conclusively. And that is precisely what the proponents, at least, would have to do. By looking at the number of murders committed while the death penalty was on the books and *enforced*, we can gain some indication of how many killers were obviously *not* deterred (because they committed murder).

However, there is absolutely no way that we can ever know, with any certainty, how many would-be murderers were in fact deterred from killing. By definition, they *were* deterred, they did *not* kill, and therefore we can never know what numbers to enter on that side of the statistical equation. We have some case histories of captured criminals (which I will later discuss) who admitted that the threat of death deterred *them.* But, for the most part, very few people who have not otherwise been embroiled with the law walk into their local precinct house and say to the desk sergeant: "Do you know, I was planning to murder my business partner but the threat of execution deterred me."

As the poet Hyman Barshay has vividly put it:

> The death penalty is a warning, just like a lighthouse throwing its beams out to sea. We hear about shipwrecks, but we do not hear about the ships the lighthouse guides safely on their way. We do not have proof of the number of ships it saves, but we do not tear the lighthouse down.[1]

Professor Charles Black of the Yale Law School, one of the nation's most ardent and articulate abolitionists, has described the problem with finality:

> . . . after all possible inquiry, including the probing of all possible methods of inquiry, we do not know, and for systematic and easily visible reasons [e.g., the impossibility of proving a negative] cannot know, what the truth about this "deterrent" effect may be. . .
>
> The inescapable flaw is . . . that social conditions in any state are not constant through time, and that social conditions are not the same in any two states. If an effect were observed (and the observed effects one way or another are not large) then one could not at all tell whether any of this effect is attributable to the presence or absence of capital punishment. A "scientific"—that is to say, a soundly based—conclusion is simply impossible and no methodological path out of the tangle suggests itself.[2]

Most of us, proponent or abolitionist alike, are forced to concede that we will never get a *conclusive* statistical picture of the deterrent effect of the death penalty. We must make do with what data we have, buttressed by a little common sense.

But before we launch into any analysis of the rather rudimentary data we do have at hand, I would like to set forth two hypothetical situations in order to point up the critical importance of the deterrence/nondeterrence argument.

Suppose that by some miracle the scientists who do things

with numbers *were* able to come up with an iron-clad conclusion on deterrence or nondeterrence, a conclusion whose statistical integrity would satisfy both proponents and abolitionists, whether or not they *liked* the conclusion.

FIRST HYPOTHETICAL CONCLUSION: *Capital punishment does not deter would-be murderers.*

This would be a major victory for the abolitionists, removing the proponents' strongest argument. Abolitionists could then say, "Since there is no deterrent effect to the penalty, and we respect the sanctity of human life, we must abolish."

The proponents could counter, "All right, there is no deterrent effect upon potential murderers, but we still believe in the death penalty to ensure that those who have been convicted of murder will not kill again. Furthermore, the death penalty is an expression of society's moral outrage at those who wantonly kill the innocent." Justice Potter Stewart, in voting to outlaw capital punishment as then applied in *Furman v. Georgia*, nevertheless said:

> When people begin to believe that organized society is unwilling or unable to impose upon criminal offenders the punishment they "deserve," then there have been sown the seeds of anarchy—of self-help, vigilante justice and lynch laws.[3]

Both sides could still hold fast to their positions in good faith.

SECOND HYPOTHETICAL CONCLUSION: *Capital punishment does deter a significant number of would-be murderers.*

This conclusion would see the proponents riding high. They could set aside their moral arguments and say, "Look, it has been proven that capital punishment deters, and the lives of innocent victims *will be saved* if we use it; let's get on with it."

The abolitionists would no longer have a leg to stand on, morally or otherwise, unless they were willing to stick to their "sanctity of human life" argument despite the known fact that if capital punishment was *not* enforced, a specified number of innocent victims would die. A highly untenable position.

Reinhold Niebuhr, the liberal theologian, said that if capital punishment were proven to be a deterrent to murder, its abolition for the sake of the principle of the sanctity of life would result in an ironical preference of the life of the guilty to that of the innocent.[4]

Of course, no clear-cut conclusion on deterrence is even remotely likely to emerge from the data; but, as the hypothetical examples demonstrate, the resolution of the dilemma has in it the seeds of the resolution of the entire capital punishment controversy.

Well, then, where does that leave us? Both sides wish to prove their case on the deterrence question; but how do they go about it?

We might draw an analogy to the manner in which cases are decided in the judicial system in the United States. There are basically two standards of proof needed to win, depending on the nature of the case: in criminal cases the state must prove the guilt of the defendant *beyond a reasonable doubt;* in civil cases the winning party must prove his case *by a preponderance of the evidence,* that is, by 51 percent or more of the evidence that a judge or jury might choose to believe.

Obviously the burden of proof for the prevailing party is much lighter in a civil case than it is for the state in a criminal case. Certainly the proponents of capital punishment should *not* have to bear the burden of proving deterrence *beyond a reasonable doubt* nor, of couse, should the abolitionists have to *disprove* deterrence beyond a reasonable doubt—neither side would be able to, anyway. The state, by definition, will have proven its case of *guilt* beyond a reasonable doubt if it convicts a murderer. The proponents and the abolitionists, in my analogy, should stand as coequal civil litigants in the "court of public opinion"; forced, because of the limitations on available data, to make their case *only* by a *preponderance of the evidence:* that good old 51 percent or more.

The term "the court of public opinion" used in the preceding paragraph is meant to include both public sentiment (which includes the two-to-one support for the death penalty in opinion polls and in the referenda in three states) *and* the policymakers in our society: the legislatures, which reflect the opinions of the majority of their constituents, and the courts, which must rule on the constitutionality and/or the legality of this reflection of

85

public opinion. Thus used, the term takes in society as a whole.

By this definition, the proponents have already won the battle of the question of deterrence in the court of public opinion. The legislatures of 35 states would not have restored the death penalty after *Furman* if they had not been convinced that it deterred murderers. They heard the evidence and they concluded that it did.

And that is their prerogative, said the Supreme Court in *Gregg v. Georgia.* Acknowledging that there is no *conclusive* evidence one way or the other, Mr. Justice Stewart nevertheless held that:

> The value of capital punishment as a deterrent of crime is a complex factual issue, the resolution of which properly rests with the legislatures, which can evaluate the results of statistical studies in terms of their own local conditions and with a flexibility of approach that is not available to the courts.[5]

Thus, on the question of deterrence the legislatures can make their own informed choices, in most instances, and the courts will not second-guess them about it. The question is so important, however, that it may be well to analyze the arguments on each side and let the reader decide which has sustained the burden of proof by a preponderance of the evidence.

First, some general reflections. The death penalty was dormant in this country from 1967, when the last man was executed, until 1977, when Gary Mark Gilmore paid the supreme penalty for murder in Utah. We have had almost a ten-year hiatus in the infliction of capital punishment. To deter a certain course of action, a threat must be perceived as real and not imaginary or illusory. During the period in which the death penalty constituted no *real* threat in the United States, the number of murders almost doubled, from roughly 10,000 to 20,000 a year.

This is not hard evidence that the threat of death, when perceived as a real threat, deterred murderers; but common sense supports the inference that if, as the threat of the death penalty decreases, the rate of murders increases, then the corollary might well be true: if the threat had increased, the homicide rate might well have decreased.

86

The phenomenon of increased murder rates once the death penalty is removed is not unique to the United States. Canada abandoned hanging in 1967, and the number of murders climbed from 281 in that year to 426 in 1971,[6] to 539 in 1974.[7] The murder *rate* in Canada increased from 1.5 per 100,000 population in 1966 to 2.3 in 1971.[8] England and Wales had 177 murders in 1971, the highest number since the death penalty was abolished in 1965.[9]

On a nonscientific basis, we learn two things from these figures: first, murder goes up when the supreme penalty is removed, which may be too simple for the statisticians but may also account for the 23-percent increase in public favor for the death penalty in the past ten years. The average citizen tends to connect cause and effect as *he* perceives them, rather than as the behavioral scientists choose to explain them to him. Second, the abolitionists did not, with all their efforts to spare human life, create a climate of good will and gratitude among potential murderers. The sanctity of everyone's life but the killers' seems to have taken a precipitate nosedive.

Another generalization. It has always been an article of faith among the abolitionists that many murders are committed by irrational people, in the heat of passion. Even if we had returned to the most *drastic* forms of capital execution—say, drawing and quartering in public—it would not deter *these* killings.

This argument is quite persuasive, but it begs the question. Capital punishment cannot and never will be able to deter *all* murderers. But this does not mean for a moment that it won't deter *any* murderers. When the criminal, particularly the murderer who *premeditates* his crime (the same murderer against whom most of the state capital murder statutes have been drawn) has an opportunity to weigh cost versus gain, cause and effect, he may well think twice if he knows that he will, in all likelihood, be put to death for his actions.

This reasoning was sufficient to satisfy the United States Supreme Court in *Gregg v. Georgia*. Justice Stewart held that:

> Although some of the studies suggest that the death penalty may not function as a significantly greater deterrent

than lesser penalties, there is no convincing empirical evidence either supporting or refuting this view.

We may nevertheless assume safely that there are murderers, such as those who act in passion, for whom the threat of death has little or no deterrent effect. But for many others, the death penalty undoubtedly is a significant deterrent. There are carefully contemplated murders, such as murder for hire, where the possible penalty of death may well enter the cold calculus that precedes the decision to act.[10]

And Potter Stewart happens to be the man whose opinion counts in such matters.

The "studies" to which Justice Stewart referred lead us into what might be called the "battle of the wizards." First the behaviorial scientists and now the economists have brought their formidable intellects to bear on the problem of deterrence, the academic solutions to which are, in many cases, diametrically opposed to each other, leading to charge and countercharge over who is right.

The behavioralists got into the act first. Criminologist Thorsten Sellin in 1959 became the Copernicus of the abolitionist movement when he compared rates of homicide per 100,000 of the population in states having the death penalty with contiguous abolition states for the period 1920–1955, including tabulations of executions in the capital punishment states. He found that the homicide rates of comparable states did not vary between those with and those without the death penalty and he concluded that "executions have no discernible effect on homicide death rates which . . . are regarded as adequate indicators of capital murder states."[11]

Sellin's findings, which were the basis of many follow-up studies reaching the same conclusion, came to be taken as dogma. People said "capital punishment doesn't deter murderers" with the same self-assurance that they might say "the earth revolves around the sun." Few people bothered to challenge Sellin's figures, and they cropped up in every abolitionist article and defendant's brief filed in the courts.

Ernest van den Haag, a testy (and brilliant) conservative professor of philosophy at New York University, was one of the few who took issue with Sellin. Van den Haag dissented on two grounds. First he said that

Professor Sellin seems to think that this lack of evidence for deterrence is evidence for the lack of deterrence. It is not. It means that deterrence has not been demonstrated statistically—not that non-deterrence has.[12]

Van den Haag also believed that Sellin's data were inadequate:

> . . .the similar areas are not similar enough; the periods are not long enough; many social differences and changes, other than the abolition of the death penalty, may account for the variation (or lack of) in homicide rates with and without, before and after abolition; some of these social differences and changes are likely to have affected homicide rates.[13]

Nevertheless, van den Haag was pretty much a voice crying in the wilderness. The findings of Sellin and his followers were taken as gospel in many quarters: It cannot be proven that capital punishment deters murder, therefore capital punishment does *not* deter murders.

Then, in the early seventies, along came a new breed: the economists. They brought the science of econometrics to bear on the study of crime and punishment, including murder, and these men began to refute the conventional wisdom. Gordon Tullock of the Virginia Polytechnic Institute at Blacksburg summed up:

> The standard criminologist has been living in a dream world for at least 150 years. They've thought that the cause of crime is not the economic-gain return sought by some people but an illness or some sort of disease. Eighty percent of the people who seriously think about crime think of punishment as a deterrent—except for the sociologists, and they wrote all the books.[14]

Tullock continued:

> Economists tend to believe that crime, far from being the result of sickness or mental disorder, in most cases is simply a business-oriented economic activity which is undertaken for the same reasons as other economic activity. To reduce the frequency of crime, economists recommend we raise the costs of crime.[15]

89

To be sure. Raise the costs of crime. What the proponents of capital punishment as a deterrent had been saying all along. And what is the highest cost that can be exacted for murder? The death penalty.

Isaac Ehrlich, professor of economics at the University of Chicago, is the dean of those who wish to apply econometrics to the crime picture. He believes that punishment deters crime; he believes that capital punishment deters capital crimes. Dr. Ehrlich is opposed to the death penalty on moral grounds but, with the integrity of the true scholar, he published in 1975 a paper entitled "The Deterrent Effect of Capital Punishment."[16] Using a mathematical technique with the forbidding name of "multiple regression analysis," he concluded, at least tentatively, that the death penalty, *if actually used* instead of imprisonment, may deter as many as eight murders *for every execution actually carried out.* Dr. Ehrlich assembled data on the frequency of murders in the United States over a period of decades; he controlled for other variables in the equation such as the consistency of enforcement of the penalty and the likelihood of capture (factors, he said, that Sellin did not control for); and he found that the death penalty had a restraining effect above and beyond all other forms of punishment.

Some writers have endorsed Dr. Ehrlich's thesis, others have criticized it sharply; one writer, though, went so far as to charge that Professor Ehrlich *understated* the matter and that

> the evidence is better consistent with the view that one execution will deter at least 50 homicides.[17]

I will frankly admit that I do not understand in full the methodology of Sellin, Ehrlich, or any of the others in the area. To the layman, a page of Professor Ehrlich's computations looks like a block of Egyptian hieroglyphics. The countless imponderables that go into a statistical "proof" of a given question make true comprehension of the methodology almost impossible. We can only report the conclusions. The academicians live in their own world and their numbers may be difficult to understand. The point, however, is that since the academicians have entered the fray we are getting at least *some* empirical data about deterrence; inconclusive, as everyone admits, but a real effort is being made by some of the best minds in the country to get a handle on the problem.*

The findings of Ehrlich, Tullock, and their fellow econometrists, whether we accept them completely or not, bring into the sharpest focus the primary principle of the deterrence argument, described briefly in the previous chapter: if we really don't know whether capital punishment deters, whose side are we to err on—the potential victims or the convicted murderers?

The question has been stated most lucidly by Professor van den Haag:

> If we do not know whether the death penalty will deter others, we are confronted with two uncertainties. If we impose the death penalty, and achieve no deterrent effect thereby, the life of a convicted murderer has been expended in vain (from a deterrent viewpoint). There is a net loss. If we impose the death sentence and thereby deter some future murderers, we spared the lives of some future victims (the prospective murderers gain, too; they are spared punishment because they were deterred). In this case, the death penalty has led to a net gain, unless the life of a convicted murderer is valued more highly than that of the unknown victim, or victims (and the non-imprisonment of the deterred non-murderer).
>
> The calculation can be turned around, of course. The absence of the death penalty may harm no one and therefore produce a gain—the life of the convicted murderer. Or it may kill future victims of murderers who could have been deterred, and thus produce a loss—their life.
>
> To be sure, we must risk something certain—the death (or life) of the convicted man, for something uncertain—the death (or life) of the victims of murderers who may be deterred. This is in the nature of uncertainty—when we invest, or gamble, we risk the money we have for an uncertain gain. Many human actions, most commitments—including marriage and crime—share this characteristic with the deterrent purpose of any penalization, and with its rehabilitative purpose (and even with the protective).[18]

If the Ehrlich thesis ever turns out to be provably correct, if one execution *could* have saved eight (or 50, or even *one*) in-

---

*An analysis of the studies and counterstudies in the area of deterrence is contained in Appendix A of this book. Appendix A is an excerpt from the brief *amicus curiae* filed by the United States in support of the state of Georgia in *Gregg v. Georgia.*

91

nocent victim, then the abolitionists may have to do some reck-
oning with their consciences.

So much for the academicians. We should thank them for,
and accord all due respect to, their hard work and their search
for the truth. But it is time to get back to the world of actual
events (again meaning no disrespect to the theoreticians).

The best way to find out if given criminals were indeed deterred from killing is to ask those criminals themselves. This
has not been done very extensively, given the natural reluctance of the average perpetrator of violent crime to discuss his
activities with the police, but some information from California
is instructive. Certain felons and would-be murderers were
willing to talk, and it seems, if they can be believed, that the
death penalty—when it was an actual, not a remote threat—deterred a lot of murders. Evidence to support this contention is
found in a study conducted by the Los Angeles Police Department in 1970 and 1971 to measure the deterrent effect of the
death penalty. Statements by persons arrested for crimes of violence were compiled. Those interviewed had been unarmed
during the commission of their crimes, or had been armed but
did not use their weapons, or had carried inoperative weapons.
Ninety-nine persons gave a statement why they went unarmed
or did not use their weapons. The results were classified as
follows:

1. Deterred by fear of death penalty from carrying weapons or operative weapon, 50 (50%).

2. Unaffected by death penalty because it was no longer
being enforced, 7 (7.07%).

3. Undeterred by death penalty, would kill whether it was
enforced or not, 10 (10.1%).

4. Unaffected by death penalty because they would not
carry weapon in any event, primarily out of fear of being
injured themselves or of injuring someone else, 32
(32.3%).[19]

Thus we see a five-to-one ratio of deterrence over nondeterrence as reported by individuals who were in the best position
to make such a judgment: the criminals themselves.

The adoption of an effectively enforced death penalty system would surely prevent some homicides. Although the death penalty had not, at the time of the study, been removed from the statute books in California, 7 percent of the suspects who were questioned believed that in reality no death penalty existed because it was not being enforced; consequently there was no deterrent. Some suspects, while realizing that the California death penalty existed in name only, admitted that the prospect of certain execution would deter them from arming themselves or using their weapons while committing crimes.

The report also notes:

> If this study contained only one and not the 50 documented cases supporting the fact that the death penalty is a deterrent, there should be no question of its retention and enforcement. In 1970 in the City of Los Angeles, 394 innocent people were victims of an unlawful execution without the right of due process of law.

Additionally, Justice Marshall McComb of the California Supreme Court (the sole dissenter in the case in which the California Supreme Court held the death penalty to be "cruel or unusual") had cited in an earlier case, as evidence of the deterrent effect of the death penalty, another series of comments from violent criminals who did not kill because of the threat of death involved for capital crimes.[20]

Here are several examples from Justice McComb's opinion that demonstrate clearly the true deterrent nature of capital punishment. In these cases lives were actually saved because a would-be killer, by his own admission, was deterred by the death penalty from murdering others in the course of a violent crime.

(a) Margaret Elizabeth Daly, of San Pedro, was arrested August 28, 1961 for assaulting Pete Gibbons with a knife. She stated to investigating officers: "Yeh, I cut him and I should have done a better job. I would have killed him but I didn't want to go to the gas chamber."

(b) Robert D. Thomas, alias Robert Hall, an ex-convict from Kentucky; Melvin Eugene Young, alias Gene Wilson, a petty criminal from Iowa and Illinois; and Shirley R. Coffee, alias Elizabeth Salquist, from California were arrested April 25, 1961 for robbery. They had used toy pistols to force their victims into a back room where the victims were bound. When the investigating officers questioned them why they used toy guns instead of genuine guns, all agreed that real guns were too dangerous, and if someone were killed in the commission of the robberies, they would all receive the death penalty.

(c) Louis Joseph Turck, alias Luigi Furchiano, alias Joseph Farino, alias Glen Hooper, alias Joe Moreno, an ex-convict with a felony record dating from 1941, was arrested May 20, 1961 for robbery. He had used guns in prior robberies in other states but only pretended to be carrying a gun in the robbery here. He told investigating officers that he was aware of the California death penalty, although he had been in the state for only one month, and when asked about the gun bluff he said: "I knew that if I used a real gun and that if I shot someone in a robbery, I might get the death penalty and go to the gas chamber."

(d) Ramon Jesse Velarde was arrested September 26, 1960 while attempting to rob a supermarket. Armed with a loaded .38 caliber revolver, he was holding several employees of the market as hostages. He subsequently escaped from jail and was apprehended at the Mexican border. While being returned to Los Angeles for prosecution, he made the following statement to the transporting officers: "I think I might have escaped at the market if I had shot one or more of them. I probably would have done it if it wasn't for the gas chamber. I'll only do 7 to 10 years for this. I don't want to die no matter what happens, you want to live another day."

(e) Orelius Mathew Steward, an ex-convict with a long felony record, was arrested March 3, 1960 for attempted bank robbery. He was later convicted and sentenced to a term in the state prison. Discussing the crime with his probation officer, he stated: "The officer who arrested me was by himself, and if I had wanted, I could have blasted him. I thought about it at the time, but I changed my mind when I thought of the gas chamber."

(f) Paul Anthony Brusseau, with a criminal record in six other states, was arrested February 6, 1960 for robbery. He readily admitted five holdups of candy stores in Los Angeles. In this series of robberies he had only pretended to be carrying a gun. When investigators asked what his reason was for simulating a gun rather than using a real one, he replied that he did not want to get the gas chamber.

(g) Salvador A. Estrada, a 19-year-old youth with a four-year criminal record, was arrested February 2, 1960, just after he had stolen an automobile from a parking lot by wiring around the ignition switch. As he was being booked at the station, he told the arresting officers: "I want to ask you one question, do you think they will repeal the capital punishment law. If they do, we can kill all you cops and judges without worrying about it."

(h) Jack Colevris, a habitual criminal with a record dating back to 1945, committed an armed robbery at a supermarket on April 25, 1960, about a week after escaping from San Quentin Prison. Shortly thereafter he was stopped by a motorcycle officer. Colevris, who had twice been sentenced, knew he would again be sent to prison for a long term. The loaded revolver was on the seat of the automobile beside him, and he could easily have shot and killed the arresting officer. According to his own statements to the interrogating officers, however, he was deterred from picking up the gun because he preferred a possible life sentence to death in the gas chamber.

(i) Edward Joseph Laplenski, who had a criminal record dating back to 1948, was arrested in December 1959 for a holdup committed with a toy automatic-type pistol. When questioned by investigators as to why he had threatened his victim with death and had not provided himself with the means of carrying out the threat, he stated, "I know that if I had a real gun and killed someone, I would get the gas chamber."

(j) George Hewitt Dixon, an ex-convict with a long felony record in the East, was arrested for robbery and kidnapping committed on November 27, 1959. Using a screwdriver in his jacket pocket to simulate a gun, he had held up and kidnapped the attendant of a service station, later releasing him unharmed. When asked why he was carrying a screwdriver instead of a real gun, this man, a hardened criminal with

95

many felony arrests and at least two known escapes from custody, indicated his fear and respect for the California death penalty: "I did not want to get the gas."

(k) Eugene Freeland Fitzgerald, alias Edward Finley, an ex-convict with a felony record dating back to 1951, was arrested February 2, 1960 for the robbery of a chain of candy stores. He used a toy gun in committing the robberies. His reason, as told to the investigating officers: "If I had a real gun and killed someone, I would get the gas, I would rather have it this way."

(l) Quentin Lawson, an ex-convict on parole, was arrested January 24, 1959 for committing two robberies, in both of which he had simulated a gun in his coat pocket. He related afterward that he did not want to kill someone and get the death penalty.

(m) Theodore Roosevelt Cronell, a man of many aliases, an ex-convict from Michigan with a criminal record of 26 years, was arrested December 31, 1958 while attempting to hold up the box office of a theater. He had simulated a gun in his coat pocket, and when asked by investigating officers why an ex-convict with everything to lose would not use a real gun, he replied, "If I used a real gun and shot someone, I could lose my life."

(n) Robert Ellis Blood, Daniel B. Grindley, and Richard R. Hurst were arrested December 3, 1958 for attempted robbery. They were equipped with a roll of cord and a toy pistol. When questioned, all of them stated that they used the toy pistol because they did not want to kill anyone, since they were aware that the penalty for killing a person in a robbery was death in the gas chamber.

Other sources give corroborating evidence that criminals fear the death penalty. Henry E. Peterson, then assistant attorney general for the criminal division of the United States Department of Justice, told the House of Representatives in 1972:

> It is not the Department's position that the death penalty deters in all cases. However, in some situations the evidence of the deterrent value of the penalty is very strong. In a study made by the American Bar Association, law enforcement officers cited the following instances where the deterrent value of the death penalty was in evidence.

(1) Criminals who had committed an offense punishable by life imprisonment, when faced with capture, refrained from killing their captors, even though it seemed likely that by killing they could have escaped. When these criminals were asked why they refrained from the homicide, they answered that they were willing to serve a life sentence, but not to risk the death penalty.

(2) Criminals about to commit certain offenses refrained from carrying deadly weapons. After their apprehension, these criminals were asked why they did not carry weapons. One of the reasons they refrained was to avoid use of such a weapon which would lead to imposition of the death penalty.

Newspapers carried the story of a prison break where an escaped convict released hostages at the State line, because, as he later told police when he was recaptured, he was afraid of the death penalty for kidnaping in the neighboring State. In the study I mentioned previously the American Bar Association reported instances where murderers have removed their victims from capital punishment States in order to avoid the threat of the death penalty. According to testimony given by the attorney general of Kansas and others before the Great Britain Royal Commission on Capital Punishment, these last-mentioned instances of murderers crossing State lines caused both Kansas and South Dakota to reintroduce the death penalty. It is the Department's position that if the threat of the death penalty deters the killing of innocent victims even to a limited extent, its retention is justified.[21]

Carol S. Vance, the district attorney of Harris County (Houston), Texas tells us:

The death penalty deterred an escape from a Texas prison. The inmate abducted a woman, stole her car, and headed west. When asked why he didn't kill this person who told police his direction of travel, [which] led to his capture, the inmate, already under a life sentence, said he didn't want to ride "Old Sparky." I have talked to robbers who said the only reason they didn't kill the only eye witness was the threat of the electric chair.[22]

These are cases in which the existence of the death penalty did deter killings. Soon after the *Furman* case was decided, an incident in New York City demonstrated that, with the death penalty no longer in effect, some people felt a significant deterrent to killing was gone. One John Wojtowicz and another held

97

eight bank employees as hostages and threatened to kill them before FBI agents captured Wojtowicz and killed his companion. In threatening to kill the hostages, Wojtowicz was explicit:

> I'll shoot everyone in the bank. The Supreme Court will let me get away with this. There's no death penalty. It's ridiculous. I can shoot everyone here, then throw my gun down and walk out and they can't put me in the electric chair. You have to have a death penalty, otherwise this can happen every day.[23]

Thanks to the aggressive action of the FBI, Wojtowicz and his companion were not able to kill any hostages, but they were certainly encouraged by the Supreme Court's leniency in *Furman*.

In March 1973 five men robbed the warehouse of the Canteen Corporation located in Landover, Maryland. They shot five of the employees and pistol-whipped eleven others after herding them into a men's room. A female employee had been shot in the throat by one of the robbers. She later testified that the robber who shot her threatened to blow all of them up with a hand grenade because there was no death penalty, so that the worst that could happen to him would be that he would be taken care of for life in prison. No hand grenade was found, but the fact that the robbers shot five people clearly indicates that since there was no death penalty for murder, they were quite willing to kill.[24]

Larry Derryberry, the attorney general of the state of Oklahoma, goes so far as to call the abolition of the death penalty *an invitation to commit murder;* and, to back up his thesis, he presents this tragic account:

> After *Furman* a striking example of the effect of the decision occurred in Oklahoma. Shortly after the decision, a young family was brutally murdered in an armed robbery of a small 24-hour grocery store in Oklahoma City. There was evidence tending to show that the killings were for the purpose of insuring that there would be no eyewitnesses to the robbery. After all, the killer had nothing to lose in taking the lives of his victims. His act of murder carried no greater punishment than his robbery of the victims by means of a firearm.[25]

Removing the death penalty can wipe out *all* deterrence to murder. Dramatic testimony to this fact is found in a letter written to Keith Sanborn, district attorney of Sedgwick County (Wichita), Kansas (a state without the death penalty), by a victim of the abolitionists' assiduous efforts on behalf of would-be murderers:

June 7, 1975

Keith Sanborn
Sedgwick County Attorney
Sedgwick County Court House
Wichita, Kansas

Dear Sir:

Will capital punishment be used again? Although we had been previously opposed to it for the usual "moral" reasons, we recently learned that our society needs it!

Last September 17th at four in the morning, three people held us captive at gun-point for three hours during an attempt to rob our bank. During that time they discussed their sentences if they were caught. They decided to kill us, rather than to leave witnesses. There wouldn't be that much difference in the "time" they would serve. They mocked the law, for we have become more concerned with the criminals' rights than those of the law-abiding citizen.

Capital punishment is *not* excessive, unnecessary punishment for those who willfully, with premeditation, set out to take the lives of others. Even though it may be used infrequently, it *does* impose a threat to the criminal.

Rosie escaped, but they shot me twice in the head and left me for dead in the bank vault. Thank God that we lived so that we can tell you that capital punishment *does* make a difference. Capital punishment will save the lives of the innocent. Our first "moral" obligations should be to the law-abiding citizen.

Sincerely yours,

MR. AND MRS. THOMAS HORNER*

Do we really need much more evidence to prove that the threat of an effective death penalty would save lives?

*Name changed to protect the privacy of the individuals.

Insofar as deterrence is concerned, we may have reached what might be termed an "empirical impasse." Yet there is considerable evidence that the proponents have met their burden of proof in the court of public opinion:

- Increased public support for capital punishment, as indicated by the surprisingly consistent two-to-one margins in referenda and public opinion polls, demonstrates a widespread belief in deterrence;
- Thirty-five state legislatures reinstated the penalty after *Furman*, which probably would not have happened if they did not perceive the threat of death as a deterrent;
- Rates of murder in this country skyrocketed once the penalty became, for all intents and purposes, defunct;
- Econometricians Ehrlich, Yunker, Tullock, and others have made a formidable statistical case for deterrence;
- Criminals themselves have said that the death penalty deterred them from killing;
- Murderers who struck while the death penalty was dormant boasted that the Supreme Court had made the decision to kill much easier;
- The Supreme Court now acknowledges that capital punishment may well be a deterrent, at least for certain classes of murderers.

On the abolitionist side we have the studies of Sellin and his colleagues, which, unlike the flat statement that capital punishment doesn't deter murderers, cannot be entirely discounted.

We could resolve the question once and for all. We could start executing murderers. Then, if we performed enough executions to make the threat of death for willful premeditated murder an actual threat again, and if the murder rate began to drop, we would be able to determine (say, over ten years) that the threat of death, when carried out, reduced the murder rate. *That* might give us some empirical data about deterrence that we could get our teeth into. Until this experiment is tried, we must concede that the deterrent arguments on either side are inconclusive. But I believe that most people agree with the rationale of Professor van den Haag, stated above: given the uncertainty of deterrence, we should resolve the question in favor of potential victims rather than convicted murderers.

Notes

1. Hyman Barshay as quoted by Ernest van den Haag, "On Deterrence and the Death Penalty," *Journal of Criminal Law, Criminology and Police Science,* vol. 60, no. 2 (1969).
2. Charles Black, *Capital Punishment: The Inevitability of Caprice and Mistake,* cited at 96 S.Ct. 2931 (1976).
3. *Furman v. Georgia,* 408 U.S. 238 at page 308 (1972) (Stewart, J., concurring).
4. Reinhold Niebuhr, *An Interpretation of Christian Ethics,* New York: Harper (1935).
5. *Gregg v. Georgia,* 428 U.S. 153, 96 S. Ct. 2909 at page 2931 (1976).
6. Eugene Griffin, "A Death Penalty Debate," *Chicago Tribune,* December 12, 1972, p. 18, sec. 1, col. 6.
7. "Crime in Canada Up Last Year," *New York Times,* May 25, 1975, p. 7, col. 1.
8. *Crime Control Digest,* February 2, 1973, p. 4.
9. "Murder In Britain at Record Since End of Death Penalty" *New York Times,* July 16, 1972, p. 5, col. 1.
10. *Gregg v. Georgia,* 428 U.S. 153, 96 S. Ct. 2909 at page 2931 (1976).
11. Thorsten Sellin, *The Death Penalty,* Philadelphia: American Law Institute (1959), p. 34.
12. Ernest van den Haag, "On Deterrence and the Death Penalty," *Journal of Criminal Law, Criminology and Police Science,* vol. 60, no. 2 (1969), reprinted in McCafferty, ed., *Capital Punishment,* Chicago: Aldine-Atherton (1972), p. 111.
13. *Ibid.,* 112. See also, Posner, "The Economic Approach to Law," 53 *Texas Law Review* 757, 766-68 (1975).
14. Michael T. Malley, "Punishment *Is* a Deterrent to Crime," *National Observer,* June 19, 1976, p. 1. col. 1.
15. *Ibid.*
16. 65 *American Economics Review* 397 (1975).
17. James Yunker, "The Deterrent Effect of Capital Punishment: Comment"; see Appendix A to this book.
18. Van den Haag, *op. cit.,* n. 12, p. 114.
19. Cited in the brief of the state of California in *Aikens v. California,* No. 68-5027 October Term, 1971, U.S. Supreme Court.
20. *People v. Love,* 56 Cal. 2d 720 (1961), McComb, J., dissenting.
21. "Controversy over Capital Punishment," *Congressional Digest,* January 1973, p. 13.
22. Carol Vance, "The Death Penalty After Furman," *The Prosecutor,* vol. 9, no. 4 (1973), p. 307.
23. Don Holloschutz, "Gunman Slain, Hostages O.K.," *Washington Star-News,* August 23, 1972, p. A-1.
24. Jim Landers, "4 Guilty in Holdup Sentence," *Washington Post,* December 8, 1973, p. B-1.
25. Larry Derryberry, "It Is the Fear That Death May Be the Punishment That Deters," *Police Digest,* Spring/Summer 1973, p. 27, col. 2.

CHAPTER 6

Incapacitation

D avid E. Kendall is a lawyer for the NAACP Legal Defense Fund, and a good one. He participated in the briefs filed by the Legal Defense Fund with the U.S. Supreme Court in the *Furman* and *Gregg* line of cases; and whether one agrees with the arguments for constitutional abolition of the death penalty made in these briefs (and despite the fact that the arguments did not, in the final analysis, prevail), they are as masterful a set of legal documents as you are likely to come across.

David Kendall was, naturally enough, not overjoyed by the Court's decisions in *Gregg, Jurek,* and *Proffitt.* His response, he told *Newsweek* magazine, would be to fight a rear-guard action, attempting to use stalling tactics and legal stratagems to keep his clients alive. "There's nothing like an execution to moot a lawsuit," he said, with a kind of mordant humor.[1]

True enough. But the proponents can turn this around: "There's nothing like an execution to moot the possibility of a second killing by a once-convicted murderer whose life has been spared."

This is what we mean by "incapacitation." Justice Byron White summed it up in his dissenting opinion in *Roberts v. Louisiana*,[2] one of the companion cases to *Gregg v. Georgia* in which the Court, by a 5–4 plurality, held that *mandatory* death sentences were unconstitutional:

> It also seems clear enough that death finally forecloses the possibility that a prisoner will commit further crimes, whereas life imprisonment does not.[3]

The abolitionists are quick to tell you that executing A for the murder of B won't bring B back to life, which is logical enough, although it underscores the contention that the victims of the crime of murder don't count for much in the abolitionist scheme of things. Except, perhaps, as an irritant. But even conceding the correctness of this proposition (and setting aside for the moment the argument that the execution of A may well deter others and will express society's outrage at the crime), if A is condemned to death and that sentence is carried out, we can be absolutely certain that he will never murder anybody else.

It is also standard abolitionist dogma that a life prison sentence, with or without possibility of parole, is as effective a deterrent as is the death penalty. And, the abolitionists add, with their never-ending but totally misplaced confidence in the essential good nature of murderers, the life sentence presents the possibility of rehabilitating the convict.

The first part of this argument has been covered in the previous chapter dealing with deterrence. Most people believe that the death penalty deters some murderers, the Supreme Court believes it deters some murderers, and there is statistical evidence that it does. Enough has been said about that.

Now, what about the life-sentence-with-possibility-of-rehabilitation argument? We can answer that on several fronts:

1. We don't know how to rehabilitate people;
2. There is no such thing as a guaranteed life sentence and probably never will be;
3. In case after case those sacred creatures—convicted murderers—have been released and have murdered

103

again, or have escaped and murdered again, or have murdered someone in prison, which should, but probably does not, give the abolitionists some real victims to think about.

Each of these elements merits discussion.

Rehabilitation is a myth. It sounds good: we take a convicted criminal and mould him, like a piece of clay, into a law-abiding, useful citizen. As generally happens, the starry-eyed people who believe in the best in all of us run headlong into a wall of facts. Rehabilitation is a good example. The thesis that we can somehow do away with punishment and simply rehabilitate criminals was analyzed by the California Governor's Select Committee on Law Enforcement Problems in 1973:

> Some fifteen years ago, a number of vocal critics of the criminal justice system attacked [the punishment of criminals] on various grounds. They said that punishment or retribution was immoral, barbaric and uncivilized. They said isolation from public protection was not justified except in extreme cases like homicidal maniacs who should be restrained only long enough to be treated. They said that punishment did not deter others from committing crimes, and even if it did it was immoral to punish a criminal to deter others from committing crimes. In their view crime was not so much a matter of individual responsibility as it was a failure of society. As a consequence they felt that the only justifiable goal of the criminal-justice system was to rehabilitate the offender so he would be able to avoid criminal behavior in the future.[4]

It might have worked, but it didn't. Recidivism rates in this country demonstrate that. As many as 65 percent of our convicted criminals sooner or later return to prison. And the reason that rehabilitation didn't work is that we don't know how to go about the business of accomplishing it, and we probably never will.

Professor Leonard Orland was quoted in Chapter 1 to the effect that we do not know enough about rehabilitation even to begin the process. A recent study in New York, conducted by the Committee for the Study of Incarceration, chaired by the ultraliberal former Senator Charles Goodell and stacked with criminal justice "progressives," found that rehabilitation did

104

not work, that we did not know how to make it work, and that perhaps we had better get back to the business of punishing criminals.[5]

A recent rather despairing article from the *New York Times* underscores the problem, as described by a corrections commissioner in Connecticut:

> After six years at the head of one of the more advanced and innovative prison systems in the country, John R. Manson, Connecticut's Commissioner of Corrections, has gradually and reluctantly come to the conclusion that the cause for rehabilitating prisoners is a lost one.
>
> With few exceptions, the Commissioner now contends, the rehabilitative approach to imprisonment, the whole framework of undeterminate sentencing, education and job training in prison, and, finally, parole, have provided a structure on which the prisoners outwit the people who imprison them and gain an easier time in prison and earlier release than society expects. "What we've got here is a facade of public protection," Mr. Manson said in an interview.[6]

Add to this the lament of Norman Carlson, Director of the Federal Bureau of Prisons: "We still live, however, with our second frustration—the inability to change the criminality of so many offenders who come into the system";[7] or the blunt warning issued by Dr. Richard A. Schwartz* to his colleagues: "Stop promoting the idea that treatment and rehabilitation programs offer a realistic hope of preventing perpetrators of serious crime from committing future crimes,"[8] and we have a fairly clear picture of the fallacy of the whole rehabilitative ideal.

Very well, so rehabilitation doesn't work. But that alone is insufficient reason to call for executions for capital murder solely on the theory that death incapacitates the individual from killing someone else. Why don't we just give murderers a life sentence and keep them inside forever so they can't harm the innocent in our society?

Because, first of all, they can and do harm other prisoners, and guards, as we will see shortly, but additionally, because there is for all intents and purposes no such thing as a "life sentence" in American prisons.

*Department of psychiatry, Cleveland Clinic Foundation, Cleveland, Ohio.

A "life sentence" in Illinois means the convict is eligible for parole in eleven years and three months (as would a sentence of 300,000 to 500,000 years under the rather permissive Illinois corrections code); even less time if the "lifer" behaves himself. In California the ante is still lower: "life" means parole eligibility after seven years.

And in some states the penalty for murder would be laughable if it didn't bring tears of rage to your eyes. In New York City, in 1975, a 15-year-old boy whose name we will never know because we don't like to stigmatize juveniles with the accusation of crime, beat an 18-year-old girl to death with a golf club as she rode her bicycle in Central Park. The judge threw the book at him: 18 months in a "rehabilitation center" (there's that word again). The lad probably perceived the penalty as harsh, but he can cheer up. Officials said that he would in all likelihood serve only six to eight months of his sentence.[9] The sentence was only one month for each year of life of his victim, but he probably will not serve much more than a third of it.

It is *that* kind of thinking that gives most of us so little faith in our criminal-justice system. And this sort of lunatic leniency is not reserved for juveniles.

Parole boards and probation authorities often laugh in the faces of judges and juries who mete out what they suppose will be "life sentences" or lengthy sentences for murder. Recall the good Dr. Geza De Kaplany, who tortured his wife to death with acid. The crime was described by Mrs. Dianne Feinstein in an article for the *San Framcisco Herald-Examiner* (See Chapter 2). She stated that

> The jury sentenced De Kaplany to "life" after testimony that the case would be given a "special (public) interest" designation which would entitle it to special consideration by the Adult Authority whose nine members would sit "en banc" (as a whole) when they considered parole.[10]

Then, Mrs. Feinstein notes, some strange things happened as the California Adult Authority paroled Dr. De Kaplany after twelve years and eight months:

> The Adult Authority itself did not hear the De Kaplany case in the March, 1975, parole hearing, but assigned it to

two staff hearing officers. Later, two Authority members rubber-stamped the release decision.

Contrary to procedure, notices of the parole hearing to be sent to interested parties (the court, district attorney and police department) for their views of parole were never sent.

Photographs of Mrs. De Kaplany's tortured body as it lay in the morgue, which were included in his file at the request of the chief of detectives to show the Adult Authority at a parole hearing ["appealing to raw emotions" again], were ordered removed from the files and have mysteriously disappeared.

One psychological report just prior to the parole hearing was written without an interview of the subject.[11]

Off went Dr. De K. to practice his medicine in Taiwan.

Even so, the Adult Authority in California was positively hard-line with De Kaplany for holding him so long. In Chapter 2 we also learned about Mrs. Lucille Miller who was convicted of drugging her husband and then burning him to death in their car. Mrs. Miller received a life sentence. She was promptly released after serving the statutory minimum of seven years.

And Lucille Miller did "hard time" compared with William P. Sweeney, whose case was also described in Chapter 2. His "infraction" was beating the police chief of Bellevue, Iowa to death with a shovel after the chief caught Sweeney and two others committing a break-in. On October 3, 1969, Sweeney pleaded guilty to second-degree murder and got 75 years for it. Two years and nine months later, "rehabilitated," he hit the street, courtesy of the Iowa Parole Board. (He was returned to prison some six months thereafter for burglary and parole violation.)

In view of cases like these, there is little wonder that the public casts a cynical eye at the general permissiveness of the criminal-justice system and at institutions like the California Adult Authority and the Iowa Parole Board in particular. "There ain't no such thing as a life sentence," they say, and vote for the death penalty.

Presumably, such a thing as a "life without possibility of parole" sentencing provision could be devised, and many judges and juries would sentence under it. But, in the long run, the public is apparently convinced that a few years down the road

the same "progressive" mentality that freed Dr. De Kaplany, Lucille Miller, and William P. Sweeney would find some loop-
hole in the statute and start cutting people loose.

And certainly the killers know about, and count on, such leniency; witness the statement of Charles Thomas Corn, a white
man, currently under sentence of death in Georgia for the
robbery-murder of a black woman. Corn, an abolitionist, was
expressing his opposition to capital punishment to a friendly
reporter: "Life imprisonment is enough for anybody. You take
seven years out of a man's life, that's a lot."[12]

A Freudian slip, perhaps, but it gives us great insight into the
thinking of at least some of the criminals on death row. Corn,
in making his statement against the death penalty, *had already
translated a life sentence into seven years in his own mind*, and
he was complaining about that! This little exercise in mental
gymnastics was glossed over by the reporter. Corn, he said, was

> referring to the minimal eligibility for parole, and not pre-
> senting the case well to those who balance the taking of a
> life against seven years.[13]

But when you think about it for a moment it's kind of scary.
At least for those of us who don't see much in the way of deterrence or incapacitation in a "life sentence." *

Now, if rehabilitation does not work, and if murderers who
are put inside have a reasonably good chance of being released
long before they should by correctional authorities who are of
the "there's no such thing as a bad boy (or girl)" persuasion,
the issue of incapacitation takes on enormous significance. **

The final question to be asked is: Will convicted murderers
who have not received the death penalty kill, or attempt to kill
again, either in prison or once they are out? The answer is important if we are to put forth incapacitation as yet another reason for imposing the death penalty.

---

*In a previous book, The Victims, New Rochelle, N.Y.: Arlington House
(1975), I examined the release of criminals and its impact on the law-abiding
public. See Chapter 5 of The Victims.
**And then we have the view of former Attorney General Ramsey Clark that
five years in prison should be the maximum term for any crime, including
murder. See Journal of the American Bar Association, vol. 63, May 1977,
p. 607. For Lance and Kelbach (Chapter 1), who murdered six on their killing spree? Five years.

And the answer is yes. Convicted murderers *have* killed again with a seemingly total lack of gratitude that their lives were spared after the first murder. National statistics on this "second murder" syndrome do not seem to be available at this time; but there are enough cases around, from different parts of the country, to indicate that the threat is a real one.

- A man named Jarrette was sentenced to a term of imprisonment in North Carolina for two separate murders. He escaped, and within two days kidnapped and raped a 16-year-old girl and robbed and murdered a 16-year-old boy.[14] Ironically, the series of decisions by the Supreme Court that upheld capital punishment in the states of Florida, Georgia, and Texas struck down statutes calling for a mandatory penalty in Louisiana and North Carolina, thus sparing Jarrette's life.
- David Pederson was convicted of murder in 1958 in New Mexico and sentenced to death. His sentence was later commuted and reduced to 14½ years. He was eventually released and within two years murdered two people in San Bernardino, California.[15] Sentenced to death in that state, he was again spared when, in December 1976, the California Supreme Court held for the second time in five years that the California death penalty was unconstitutional.[16]
- Fredrick Burson and Joseph Bowen, both convicted for the murder of police officers, stabbed to death Deputy Warden Robert Fromhold and Chief Administrative Officer Patrick V. Curran at Holmesburg Prison in Philadelphia in May of 1973.[17]
- In Philadelphia, during the year 1972, *fifteen* persons with prior arrests for murder were again arrested—for murder.[18]
- In 1971 a parolee from the Indiana State Penitentiary shot and killed an Indiana state policeman who was attempting to arrest him for another murder committed three days earlier. The man was free on parole after serving 21 months of a two-to-twenty-one-year sentence for voluntary manslaughter.[19]
- In August of 1972, at Norfolk County Prison near Boston, Massachusetts, a convicted murderer killed two prison employees, his wife, and himself in an escape attempt.[20]
- Alfred Ravenell had been sentenced to death for three murders in New Jersey. His sentence was commuted and on October 14, 1972 he was at liberty to murder a Pennsylvania state trooper.[21]

109

And, finally, a series of cases from California gives further evidence that murderers who are spared *will* kill again.

People v. Purvis, 52 Cal. 2d 871 346 P. 2d 22 (1959)

In 1950 defendant was convicted of second-degree murder of his wife and sentenced to prison. In 1954 he was paroled. In 1957 he murdered a woman and was convicted, with the death penalty imposed. The California Supreme Court affirmed judgment but ordered a retrial on issue of penalty.

People v. Gilbert, 63 Cal. 2d 690, 408 P. 2d 365 (1965)

Gilbert was convicted in 1947 of second-degree murder for killing a fellow prisoner at San Quentin. He was released on parole in 1959 and convicted of burglary in 1960. He escaped in 1965 and committed a series of armed bank robberies. In 1964 he killed a police officer while committing a bank robbery. Gilbert was convicted of first-degree robbery and kidnapping and received the death penalty.

People v. Robles, 2 Cal. 3d 205, 466 P. 2d 710 (1970)

Robles was serving a life sentence for first-degree murder. He had a prior conviction for assault with intent to commit murder. While in prison, he murdered an inmate by striking him on the head and cutting his throat from ear to ear. Robles was convicted of first-degree murder and received the death penalty. The California Supreme Court reversed the penalty.

People v. St. Martin, Cal. 3d 524, 463 P. 2d 390 (1970)

Defendant was serving a life sentence for second-degree murder and robbery in the first degree. While a guard was trying to restrain him, defendant plunged a knife three times into an inmate's chest, killing him. Defendant was convicted and given the death penalty. The California Supreme Court reversed the judgment.

People v. Peete, 28 Cal. 2d 306 (1946)

Defendant was convicted of murder in 1921 and after 18 years was released from prison. In 1944 defendant murdered another person and this time received the death penalty.

People v. Hall, 199 Cal. 451 (1926)

Hall escaped from prison while serving a life sentence for murder. Subsequently he committed another murder and was convicted and received the death penalty. The California Supreme Court reversed judgment.

110

People v. Morse, 70 Cal. 2d 711 (1969)

Morse, serving a sentence of life imprisonment for two murders, garroted a fellow prisoner who owed him some cigarettes. Sentenced to death for this murder, Morse got the judgment reversed by the California Supreme Court.

We can reasonably assume that the foregoing histories of "second murders" are not isolated instances. No sentence except death can ensure that further innocent victims will not be murdered by those who might have been executed the first time. The net result is that any number of people are now dead because the incapacitation feature of the death penalty was not utilized.

The incapacitation argument may not be the principal argument made by the proponents, but it carries considerable weight. In the words of the then solicitor general of the United States, Robert Bork, who filed a brief as a friend of the court in support of the death penalty in *Gregg v. Georgia:*

> We would scarcely argue that the need to incapacitate certain offenders is a good ground for the execution of all offenders. But offenders may by their actions become open to capital punishment under this rationale, perhaps after committing second murders. In any event, this justification for capital punishment, like the other justifications, does not stand alone. It is cumulative with the others; together, even if not separately, they indicate that legislatures rationally could decide that capital punishment is an appropriate response to some crimes.[22]

Without a doubt, the legislatures *did* weigh the factor of incapacitation in the balance when deciding to restore the death penalty, and they apparently believed that it was an important factor. "Second murders" are the one class of cases that the abolitionists can't talk their way around. A murders B; he should have been executed but was not. A is then released and kills C; or he escapes and kills C; or, while in prison, he murders C. C's death is a direct consequence of the failure to do away with A, and no amount of gibberish about the sanctity of human life can get around that fact.

There is nothing like an execution to prevent a second murder.

Notes

1. Jerrold Footlick and Lucy Howard, "Dusting Off Old Sparky," *Newsweek*, November 29, 1976, p. 35. col. 1.
2. 428 U.S. 325 (1976) (White, J., dissenting).
3. *Ibid.*, at page 3016.
4. "Controlling Crime in California," Report of the Governor's Select Committee on Law Enforcement Problems, Sacramento, Calif., August 1973, p. 66.
5. "Abandon Rehabilitation as Goal of Sentencing, Committee Urges," *Crime Control Digest*, February 23, 1976, p. 4, col. 1.
6. Lawrence Fellows, "Prison Program Called a Failure," *New York Times*, June 1, 1976, p. 20, col. 3.
7. Norman Carlson, "Remarks Before the Correctional Seminar of the University of Miami," Miami, Florida, February 2, 1973, p. 2.
8. Richard Schwartz, M.D., "Psychiatry and Crime Control," *Diseases of the Nervous System*, vol. 36, February 1975, p. 59.
9. "New York Youth Gets 18 Months in Death of Girl," *Chicago Tribune*, November 1, 1975, sec. 1, p. 7, col. 1.
10. Dianne Feinstein, "Life Prison Sentences That Would Mean No Parole," *San Francisco Herald-Examiner*, March 12, 1976, p. 35, col. 1.
11. *Ibid.*
12. Pat Watters, "Death Row, Three Who Wait," *Juris Doctor*, vol. 7, no. 1, January 1977, p. 25.
13. *Ibid.*
14. *State v. Jarrette*, 284 N.C. 625.
15. Editorial, "Death Row Jubilation," *Los Angeles Hearld-Examiner*, December 9, 1976, p. A-14, col. 1.
16. *Rockwell v. Superior Court (People)*, No. LA 30645, December 7, 1976, Cal. Sup. Ct.
17. Frank Rizzo, "Bring Back Capital Punishment," *Argosy*, September 1973, p. 38, col. 1.
18. *Ibid.*, p. 59.
19. J. Edgar Hoover, testimony before the Committee on Appropriations, United States House of Representatives, March 2, 1972.
20. Bill Kovach, "2 Slain by Convict in Break Attempt," *New York Times*, August 1, 1972, p. 18.
21. Letter: Lancaster County, Pennsylvania district attorney's office to William R. Powell, Philadelphia district attorney's office, August 22, 1973.
22. Brief *amicus curiae* of the United States, *Gregg v. Georgia*, No. 74-627, October Term, 1975, Supreme Court of the United States, p. 51.

CHAPTER 7

Arbitrary and Discriminatory?

The abolitionists could count. They knew that if they wanted to win the case of *Furman v. Georgia*, they would have to get five votes, and that was about as much as they could expect. For openers, they knew it was most improbable that they could convince Chief Justice Warren Burger or Justices Lewis F. Powell and William H. Rehnquist to vote for abolition. The three were hard-liners on the law and order issue.

They knew that Justice Harry A. Blackmun was on record as opposing the death penalty *personally*, but in judicial philosophy he may be the most conservative jurist on the Court.* One of the principal tenets of judicial conservatism is that the courts are not supposed to meddle in matters that are properly the province of the legislative branch, and Justice Blackmun could

---

*That is why a lot of jaws dropped when Justice Blackmun wrote the *Roe v. Wade* abortion-on-demand decision. It was out of character for him to venture so far into judicial legislation.

113

be expected to vote that way (which he did, despite his personal opinions).

On the plus side, the abolitionists knew that they could count on the votes of Justices William O. Douglas, William J. Brennan, and Thurgood Marshall, the three remaining liberal justices from the "Warren Court" which between 1960 and 1969 reversed 63 of 112 federal criminal convictions and 113 of 144 state convictions.[1] They weren't about to vote for anything that might tend to strengthen victims' rights against the rights of accused or convicted criminals; and each had proven himself more than willing to substitute his personal judgments and predilections for the will of the elected representatives of the people.

So the head count was 4–3 against the abolitionist position. This left Potter Stewart, appointed to the Court by President Eisenhower in 1958, and Byron R. White, appointed by President Kennedy in 1962, as the "swing men." Both justices were considered conservative on criminal-justice issues and each had dissented bitterly from many of the Warren Court decisions that revolutionized the criminal law in favor of the defendant.* However, both men, extremely intelligent and thoughtful jurists, are rather flexible in their conservatism. They cannot be pinned down. They might be unwilling to throw out the death penalty forever as constituting cruel and unusual punishment under the Eighth Amendment, but if they could be convinced that the penalty *as applied* was either arbitrary—i.e., randomly and capriciously invoked—or discriminatory—i.e., inflicted disproportionately on racial minorities—or both, then they might be willing to hold it unconstitutional.

The abolitionists knew that the "arbitrary" and "discriminatory" argument might well be their strongest. It was one of their basic arguments; the one that eventually prevailed in *Furman*. Professor Anthony Amsterdam, arguing for the abolitionist side, told the Court that in most states juries had a wide discretion in recommending either death or some lesser penalty, and according to the available evidence, this discretion was exercised randomly and capriciously.[2]

---

*See, e.g., Justice White's dissent in *Miranda v. Arizona*, 384 U.S. 436 (1966), in which Justice Stewart joined. Noted above at page 75.

114

He pointed out that juries return about 100 death verdicts each year, a ratio of one such verdict for every 12 or 13 cases in which the death penalty *could* have been invoked. This, he said, proved that the penalty was not uniformly applied, and any penalty not uniformly applied would violate the Eighth Amendment to the Constitution.

Capital punishment was arbitrarily and selectively applied to "a few outcast pariahs," notably the ugly, the poor, and the black. Counsel cited statistics to demonstrate that black people received the death penalty more often than did whites for rape and other crimes—hence the death penalty was not only arbitrary but it discriminated against minorities.

It was a good argument and it won the case for the abolitionists. The vote was 5−4. The majority was composed of Justices Brennan and Marshall, who felt that capital punishment was *per se* cruel and unusual; Justice Douglas, who believed that the inherent discrimination against minorities in the penalty rendered it unconstitutional; and, as hoped for, Justices Stewart and White, who bought the "arbitrary and capricious" argument completely.

Justice Stewart found that current death penalty legislation provided no guidance on when the sanction should be used to deter the crimes for which it was imposed. Few defendants incurred it, while a capriciously selected handful did. He concluded that

> These death sentences are cruel and unusual in the same
> way that being struck by lightning is cruel and unusual.[3]

Justice White stated his view that the very infrequency of the application of the penalty rendered it useless as a deterrent or as a means of retribution, hence it was cruel and unusual. But he, like Justice Stewart, used the words "as it is presently administered,"[4] a phrase that was destined to come back to haunt the abolitionists.

In the last section of this book we will examine the *Furman* and *Gregg* decisions in detail: how and why the justices were asked to rule and how and why they *did* rule. At this point we need to look a little more closely at the arbitrary and discriminatory arguments, for the obvious reason that these arguments won the *Furman* case; but perhaps more importantly because they do indeed present very serious questions about our criminal-justice system.

We want the system to be *fair*. We need to protect ourselves from the ever-increasing depredations of criminals, but we want to be fair to the accused and even the convicted criminal in so doing. Can we really say that we are acting in fairness if two convicted criminals in different cases receive such widely disparate sentences that the only conclusion that can be reached is that the system is arbitrary and capricious?

No, said the *Furman* majority, at least insofar as the death penalty is concerned: that is not fair, and what is not fair is unconstitutional.

But, if a penalty is so arbitrarily applied as to make it unconstitutional, the answer is not, as the abolitionists suggest, to do away with it altogether, but to refine our standards so that the penalty is not applied in an arbitrary manner. That is precisely what the states set out to do; successfully, as matters turned out.

The legislators of Florida, Georgia, and Texas took a long, hard look at the crime of murder. First they decided which kinds of murder were so horrifying, so aggravated, so shocking to the conscience that they could be properly classified as capital murder. This classification was a first step towards eliminating arbitrariness: no longer will a man who coldly and calculatedly guns down a liquor store clerk in the course of a robbery so that he will not be around to testify against him, or one who murders a policeman to avoid being captured, receive the same penalty as, say, someone who shoots his wife in a fit of jealous rage or who gets into a drunken cutting-scrape over a crap game.

The second step taken by the three states whose capital punishment statutes were upheld was to reduce further the chance of arbitrary infliction of the death penalty by providing for a case-by-case review of such verdicts, thus ensuring that the offense fit into one or more classes of capital murder, that the defendant was actually guilty of the crime, that the punishment was not disproportionate to the offense, and finally, that no prejudice of any kind caused the sentence of death.

This second step was considered to be of extreme importance by a majority of the Supreme Court. The Court struck down the capital punishment laws of states that, by making the death penalty *mandatory* for certain classes of crimes, failed to provide the same sort of thoroughgoing case-by-case review that rendered the Florida, Georgia, and Texas schemes constitutional in the eyes of the Court.

The abolitionists, with their usual consistency, argued in the *Gregg* series of cases that, notwithstanding the efforts of the legislators to come up with an even-handed method of dealing out capital sentences, the Florida, Georgia, and Texas statutes *still* remained arbitrary and discriminatory.

The argument wouldn't wash the second time around. Potter Stewart, who found the whole death penalty apparatus arbitrary in *Furman*, told them that enough was enough. The abolitionist argument seemed to be that if there was *any* discretion reposed in *anyone*—prosecutor, judge or jury—the case for capital punishment must fall.

No, Justice Stewart said, the states did what we asked them to do in *Furman*. They got rid of the arbitrary features as much as anyone living in this imperfect world can do. They have classified the offenses properly, and provided adequate protections in the process of review of capital sentences. We're going to O.K. this batch.

The question of racial discrimination in the infliction of the death penalty looms large. We cannot deny that racial minorities were oppressed and discriminated against in this country for years. In the area of capital punishment, this discrimination was particularly invidious.

Jack Greenberg, an abolitionist attorney who argued in the *Furman* series of cases before the Supreme Court, told the Court that, before the Civil War, the death penalty was mandated if a black raped a white woman; but if any other combination was involved, the sentence was one to twenty years.[5] This was racial discrimination with a vengeance.

Things calmed down somewhat after the Civil War, but one

117

must concede that in the past our system of justice was, in some localities, tainted with racial prejudice. The question then arises: Is race a factor in the administration of justice today? And, in particular, is there racial prejudice in the area of capital punishment?

The solicitor general of the United States, in his "friend of the court" brief in Gregg v. Georgia, submitted to the Court his opinion that racial discrimination in capital sentencing does not, or at least cannot be proven to, exist today.* Citing the most recent and sophisticated study,[6] he stated that it "found no evidence whatever of racial discrimination in capital punishment for murder."[7]

It is certainly true that the arrest rate of blacks for murder and death sentences of blacks for murder are high. Blacks are involved in 57 percent of all arrests for murder; between 50 and 60 percent of all death sentences for murder are meted out to blacks. Such figures would make a case for discrimination in the capital murder process,[8] unless we take into consideration the fact that, while blacks make up about 12 percent of our population, black people are the *victims* of murder in fully 50 percent of all homicide cases.[9]

The *Dallas Morning News* summed up this situation rather succinctly in a recent editorial:

> The traditional civil rights argument has held that the death penalty is discriminatory in that it falls disproportionately on poor blacks. It's true that the penalty is statistically more likely to be carried out on blacks than their proportion of the population would indicate. But the killers' civil rights are not the only civil rights involved in these cases.
>
>   *   *   *
>
> ... consistently overlooked in all of the battle over the death penalty is the share of black victims. The number of black crime victims far outweighs the number of black criminals, let alone the number of blacks under a death sentence, yet there seems to be little concern for them by those individuals and organizations that profess to be protecting black rights.

*His arguments are set forth in Appendix B to this book.

The chief prey of the typical black criminals is other blacks. Don't these victims and potential victims have rights, too?[10]

And it is clear beyond cavil that black people and other racial minorities who live in our inner cities are the principal victims of crime in America, at a rate so disproportionate that it is, or should be, considered a matter of national disgrace.

The late Professor Herbert Packer of Stanford University reported in 1970 that inner-city dwellers were at least 100 times more likely to be victims of violent crime than were middle-class whites living in the suburbs.[11] An Associated Press survey in August of 1970 reported that 70 to 80 percent of big-city crime occurred in black or predominantly black districts.[12]

Newsweek magazine covered the topic of minorities as victims of crime in its edition of December 18, 1970. It noted:

What middle-class people frequently forget is that poor people—especially poor black people—have been living with the same fears and worse for a long time. Parthenia Waters won't venture out after dark from her three-room public housing flat in Chicago's Wentworth police district, where one out of every 27 persons last year was the victim of violent crime: murder, rape, robbery or assault. "Whatever you need and can't borrow from a neighbor just has to wait until the next day," Mrs. Waters explains. All through the night, she stands guard behind the door. "Sometimes I doze off for an hour and then I wake up," she says. "From then till morning I'm walking the floor, listening. I'm so scared somebody might come in here on us. I don't know what I'd do if somebody did." In the morning, she keeps her 12-year-old in the apartment until precisely 8:50 A.M., when the doors of the nearby school are opened, then sees her off from the project's outdoor ramp.

The atmosphere is similarly oppressive in most ghettos. "It's heart-breaking to see what this city has become," sighs a 70-year-old Harlem woman who was mugged last month. "I used to enjoy playing bridge with my friends, but we haven't done that in a year. I used to look forward to the evening Lent services, but that's finished." Ironically, even those who break out into middle-class black neighborhoods remain prime targets for black criminals, who realize they can be spotted more quickly in white

119

areas. "I live in constant fear now," says Mrs. Lennon Harris, whose husband just spent $1,000 fortifying their Memphis home after a $3,800 burglary. "You work and save so you can have nice things, then some punk just comes in and takes it away from you."

Now then, though there seems to be little evidence that capital punishment discriminates against blacks, there is overwhelming evidence that *crime—and murder particularly*—hits blacks (and other racial minorities) hardest. This was made crystal clear by Illinois State Senator Raymond Ewing, a black, who in 1971 refused to vote for a proposed moratorium on capital punishment. His reasoning: "I realize that most of those who face the death penalty are poor and black and friendless. I also realize that most of their victims are poor and black and friendless and dead."[13]

If capital punishment deters, or at least incapacitates, murderers, and if blacks account for 50 percent of our murder victims, then its abolition would be the last thing in the world that we would want to do if we have a decent concern for the poor and powerless.

An analogy: In 1968 the Supreme Court had before it the question of whether the police practice of "stop and frisk," that is, stopping persons suspected of criminal activity in public places, asking them to account for what they were doing, and patting them down for weapons, was constitutional.

Those opposing "stop and frisk" urged upon the Court the suggestion that the practice discriminated against blacks. James R. Thompson, then a professor of law at Northwestern University, now governor of Illinois, in a friend-of-the-court brief filed on behalf of Americans for Effective Law Enforcement, Inc., turned the argument around. As a strong and sympathetic advocate of blacks as victims, he said:

> The police could, of course, withdraw from the ghetto.... This alternative might be somewhat tolerable if only criminals lived in the ghetto; at least *their* interferences with human liberty in the form of murder, rape, robbery and other crimes would be practiced on each other. But others live in the ghetto as well—innocent, law-abiding American citizens, by far the overwhelming major-

120

ity. They are entitled under the ... Constitution of the
United States to live their lives and experience the safety
of their homes and their streets without fear of criminal
marauders. They have suffered enough—discrimination,
poverty, lack of education, appalling conditions of aliena-
tion. Must they also be deprived of the protection of the
law as well?

This may be one of the reasons why the Court voted 8–1
to uphold the practice of "stop and frisk."

Capriciousness and arbitrariness in our system of justice
must be eradicated, to the extent possible. Likewise discrimination in all its forms, but especially racial discrimination.

Both existed at one time. We are trying to eliminate them. In
the Gregg series of capital punishment cases we seem to have
done so.

The Supreme Court of the United States, in its decisions in
Gregg, Jurek, and Proffitt, seems to have foreclosed the notion
that, because there is some inevitable discretion reposed in
judges, prosecutors, and jurors in capital murder cases, the
death penalty is unconstitutionally "arbitrary." Nevertheless,
we must concede that such discretion exists and, additionally,
that the possibility of mistake is inherent in any discretionary
function.

This concession leads us directly into a confrontation with
the "we might execute an innocent man" theory that the abolitionists put forth as yet another reason for doing away with the
death penalty.

Van den Haag, while by no means agreeing with this conclusion, sums up the proposition with his customary lucidity:
"... though (nearly) all penalties are irreversible, the death
penalty, unlike others, is irrevocable as well."[14]

It is indeed; quite obviously. We can return his money to a
man who was wrongly fined, and we can at least try to compen-
sate an individual who was wrongly convicted and served
time, but we most assuredly cannot bring an innocent man back
to life who has been executed by mistake.

To the purists, to those who solemnly say, "I would rather
one hundred (or one thousand, or whatever) guilty persons go

free than convict one innocent person," this possibility standing alone would be enough to outlaw capital punishment forever.

But matters are more complicated than that. The average citizen who has just been hit on the head by one of those hundred guilty persons, or who lives in a constant, and reasonable, fear of being hit on the head by the same, has little use for such theorizing.

Nor does the great majority of the public have much fear of being wrongly convicted and executed. If this possibility were perceived as a real threat, we would never see the public opinion polls showing such high rates of acceptance for capital punishment as they do. The public desires protection against the *criminal*, not the executioner.

Still we must confront the *possibility* of the execution of the innocent. The response of the proponent of capital punishment is threefold: statistically the possibility is remote to the point of insignificance; legally the possibility is remote; and the benefits of the use of the death penalty—deterrence, retribution, incapacitation, and so on—far outweigh the possibility of execution in error.

There is no question but that we should shudder in horror if an innocent man is executed. But we must ask whether this threat is an actual or merely a hypothetical one. William O. Hochkammer, Jr., writes that

> abolitionists have been unable to show many instances in which it had been established that an innocent person actually was executed, although they have pointed to numerous cases in which persons sentenced to prison were later found to be innocent.[15]

Sarah R. Ehrmann, who is the former executive director of the American League to Abolish Capital Punishment, which gives some idea of where she stands on the issue, wrote a long, thoughtful, and (from her point of view) well-researched article calling for the abolition of capital punishment.[16]

In the article she dwells at some length on the possibility of executing the innocent. She documents, dramatically, some dozen cases in the United States of persons sentenced to death for murder but who, for one reason or another, usually commu-

122

tation, were not executed and whose innocence was later proven.

She documents only one case, however, of an innocent man who was actually *executed* in this country: one Jack O'Neill who, in 1898, was hanged for a murder to which a dying soldier later confessed.

One can certainly sympathize with these innocents who spent months or years in prison, under the shadow of death, for crimes they did not commit. We wish we could rid our system of such imperfections. But we can't; because, being human, we are bound to make mistakes on occasion. The only way to avoid such tragedies would simply be to cease prosecuting for murder.

But the fact that Mrs. Ehrmann could cite to us only one case of actual execution of the innocent in the United States, and that one 78 years ago, indicates that the possibility of such a miscarriage is remote to nonexistent. In actuality, Mrs. Ehrmann's case histories of persons sentenced to death *but who were not executed* (and later proven innocent) demonstrate that our legal system examines capital convictions with such an intense scrutiny that, as in these cases, when there is the slightest doubt of guilt (even after conviction), a commutation will usually result, or the individual will otherwise be spared, thus lessening the chance of executing the innocent.

Our legal system bends over backward to ensure that the innocent are not convicted. So many procedural safeguards are built into it that, with the exception of a few cases such as Mrs. Ehrmann cited, we can say with reasonable certainty that we will convict *only* the guilty.

The accused is entitled to counsel at every step of the proceedings; free counsel if he cannot afford a lawyer.* He has the right to confront his accusers and to obtain full discovery of

---

*We often hear that only the poor are sentenced to death because the rich can afford a battery of high-priced lawyers to get them off. That may have been true years ago, but it is not so now. Some of the brightest and most aggressive attorneys in the country spend their careers working for the poor for no fee: in public defenders' offices, for civil rights and civil liberties groups, and so on. I doubt, for example, that Professor Amsterdam presented much of a bill for legal fees to Messrs. Furman, Gregg, Proffitt, Jurek, Woodson, or Roberts; yet all the combined wealth of the Rockefellers could not have purchased finer legal representation.

123

their testimony and other evidence against him prior to trial. He can testify in his own behalf if he wishes, or, if he decides not to, the prosecutor may not comment, directly or indirectly, on his silence.

All evidence favorable to the accused that comes to the knowledge of the prosecutor must be made available to him.

Evidence against him that was obtained by the police in any manner that violated his rights cannot be used: physical evidence, if obtained by "illegal search and seizure"; confessions, if found to be involuntary or made in the absence of specific assurances of his right to remain silent and his right to have an attorney present; and so on.

Jury verdicts in capital cases must be unanimous. The evidence must persuade the jury beyond a reasonable doubt. Appeals to every level of the judicial system are available, the convicted defendant is entitled to free counsel, and a free copy of transcripts of proceedings must be made available to him if desired.

With this panoply of procedural safeguards, it can hardly be said that the risk of convicting the innocent is great. And in capital cases the strictures to avoid error and mistake are drawn even tighter. Review of a death sentence is automatic and painstaking. The Georgia scheme of review in such cases requires:

1. Upon a guilty verdict or plea of guilty in a capital case, a separate hearing is held to determine the penalty. The jury hears evidence in aggravation *and* mitigation.
2. At least one of ten aggravating circumstances must be found by the jury or judge beyond a reasonable doubt and designated in writing before a death sentence can be pronounced.
3. Review of the death sentence by the Georgia Supreme Court is automatic. The court must consider whether the sentence was influenced by passion, prejudice, or any other arbitrary factor, the evidence must support the finding of aggravation, and the sentence must not be disproportionate, and, finally, if the court upholds the death sentence, it must refer to similar cases that it has considered.[17]

In short, the mills of criminal justice in the United States grind exceedingly fine. It is *possible* for an erroneous death sentence to filter through the mesh of legal safeguards, but the likelihood can be considered remote at best. As Hochkammer has noted:

> But since the death penalty is in fact imposed for only those capital crimes which shock the public, where guilt is clear, and in light of the existing safeguards of appellate review and the possibility of commutation, execution of the innocent is unlikely.[18]

The "innocent man" theory is, as we have noted, speculative at best. When we add the fact that, at least for those who believe in the efficacy of deterrence and incapacitation in saving the lives of innocent victims, the death penalty has a definite value for society, the "innocent man" argument becomes almost negligible. Or as van den Haag has put it:

> If the death of innocents because of judicial error is unjust, so is the death of innocents by murder. If some murders could be avoided by a penalty conceivably more deterrent than others—such as the death penalty—then the question becomes: which penalty will minimize the number of innocents killed (by crime and by punishment)?[19]

The proponents of capital punishment believe that its application will minimize the number of innocents killed by murderers. It's as simple as that.

Notes

1. *Congressional Record*, August 11, 1969, p. 9565. Remarks of Senator John L. McClellan (D-Ark.).
2. This and subsequent excerpts from the arguments in *Furman* are based upon an account of the oral argument in *The Criminal Law Reporter*, January 2, 1972, vol. 10, p. 4146.
3. 408 U.S. 238 at page 309.
4. *Ibid.*, at page 312.
5. *Criminal Law Reporter, op. cit.*, p. 4149.
6. "A Study of the California Penalty Jury in First-Degree-Murder Cases: Standardless Sentencing," 21 *Stanford Law Review* 1297 (1969).
7. Brief *amicus curiae* of the United States in *Gregg v. Georgia*, p. 65.
8. *Ibid.*, p. 66–67.
9. *Ibid.*

10. Editorial, "What About Victims," *Dallas Morning News,* July 24, 1976.
11. *Crime Control Digest,* March 25, 1970, p. 7.
12. "Black Crime Preys on Black Victims," *Denver Post,* August 23, 1970, p. 35. See generally: Frank Carrington, *The Victims,* New Rochelle, N.Y.: Arlington House (1975), Chapter 2; Parker and Brownfeld, *What the Negro Can Do About Crime,* New Rochelle, N.Y.: Arlington House (1974).
13. "Ban Death Penalty, State House Unit Urges," *Chicago Tribune,* April 13, 1971, p. 1.
14. Van den Haag, "On Deterrence and the Death Penalty," *Journal of Criminal Law, Criminology and Police Science* vol. 60, no. 2 (1969), reprinted in McCafferty, ed., *Capital Punishment,* Chicago: Aldine-Atherton (1972), p. 104.
15. William O. Hochkammer, Jr., "The Capital Punishment Controversy," *Journal of Criminal Law, Criminology and Police Science* vol. 60, no. 3 (1969), reprinted in McCafferty, ed., *op. cit.,* p. 70.
16. Sarah R. Ehrmann, "For Whom the Chair Waits," *Federal Probation Quarterly,* March 1962, Administrative Office of the United States Courts, pp. 14–25.
17. From the Syllabus to *Gregg v. Georgia,* 96 S. Ct. 2909 at page 2916 (1976).
18. Hochkammer, *op. cit.,* p. 71.
19. Van den Haag, *op. cit.,* p. 104.

CHAPTER 8

The Moral Arguments

The writer looks at a clean page and he knows that he could write a thousand words or a hundred million words about the moral aspects of capital punishment—pro or con—and still not shed much more light than has already been shed on the subject.

This is understandable. When we talk about other issues—deterrence, incapacitation, and so on—at least we have *something* concrete to talk about, even if we cannot reach definitive conclusions. We have *some* numbers, for example, on the question of deterrence—Sellin, Bedau, *et al.*: "The death penalty doesn't deter"; Ehrlich, Tullock, *et al.*: "If enforced, it does deter." We have the case histories, cited in Chapter 5, where potential murderers *said* they were deterred, and we have the cases of "second murders" described in Chapter 6. Neither side has *proven* anything to the satisfaction of the other (and probably never will), but there are *some* data, rudimentary and fragmentary as they may be.

When we leap up to the plane of moral arguments about the

subject, however, we have no physical data to get our teeth into, only the differing philosophical views of the proponents and abolitionists. Both groups are going to stick to their positions with the tenacity of a young puppy clenching a slipper in his teeth in spite of his master's best efforts to get it back. Nothing short of an atom bomb, for example, is going to dislodge Ernest van den Haag from his unshakable belief that "the inviolability of human life is proclaimed and protected by the credible threat of death" for anyone who takes a human life, willfully and premeditatedly.[1] Nor Ira Schwartz of the John Howard Association, who tells us with an equally rocklike adherence to his principles that "society teaches us that human life is to be valued, that to kill is wrong, and yet society and the state sanction the crime of *murder* . . ." (my emphasis) by executing criminals.[2]

Van den Haag would then patiently explain to Schwartz:

> Murder is an unlawful killing, just as stealing is an unlawful taking. Lawful execution is not murder any more than lawful confiscation is stealing.[3]

And so on.

Each is dealing on a philosophical level. They're not talking about statistics or actual cases or any of that mundane jazz. The argument, although heated, is an exercise in theoretical arm-wrestling. And there is no more possibility of one convincing the other to change his view than there is of overcoming the laws of physics; the irresistible force has met the immovable object.

Then why bother to talk about moral aspects of capital punishment if the philosophers are merely playing an arcane game somewhere off in the empyrean realms? The reason is that although the van den Haags and the Schwartzes may never convince each other, and there is little that is new in the battle of the philosophers, the moral arguments for and against capital punishment carry a lot of weight with some of the policymakers in our society, notably the Supreme Court of the United States.

A case in point: in *Furman v. Georgia*, the abolitionists relied heavily on the premise that "standards of decency" had "evolved" to such an extent that the Eighth Amendment should be construed by the Court to prohibit execution for any crime, regardless of its depravity or impact on society. This argument is entirely theoretical and speculative, but two justices, Brennan and Marshall, bought it and the abolitionists won.

Additionally, the moral arguments may soon take on an increased importance, at least for the abolitionists. We may soon have an opportunity to see whether capital punishment really deters murderers. The *Gregg* line of decisions upheld the death penalty in three states and provided a blueprint for any other states that may want to enact statutes that will pass constitutional muster. It seems likely that we will see other states, like Utah, begin to execute people for committing particularly horrible murders.

Now, if a given state, say Georgia, enforces the penalty for a given number of years, and if murder rates in Georgia decline significantly (and almost *any* decline would be significant because it would mean the saving of innocent lives), then we will have gone a long way toward proving that the enforced threat of death *is* a deterrent.

What a happy state of affairs that would be for the proponents! It is always nice to be proven right, of course, on *any* issue; but how much nicer to be proven right while saving human lives.

But the same state of affairs will not be such a happy one for the abolitionists, drawing, as it will, the sting from their arguments that death does not deter. They will, of course, come up with any number of ways of proving that an increase-in-execution/decrease-in-murder ratio doesn't mean a thing. Common sense being what it is, however, most people will not buy that sort of argument and capital punishment will definitely be perceived as a deterrent.

Now, admittedly the foregoing is iffy. It relies on a series of events that may or may not occur. But *if* it does come about, then the abolitionists are going to be left with *only* their "moral" arguments to sustain their position. If for no other reason than that, we should examine their arguments (and the counterarguments to them).

From a review of abolitionist literature,[4] their "moral" arguments can be summarized thus: a) human life is sacred so we should not execute murderers; b) "evolving standards of decency" render capital punishment cruel and unusual; and c) society has no right to exact retribution for antisocial acts.

Ramsey Clark, the perennial (and unsuccessful) candidate for high public office in the state of New York, has as great a capacity for ignoring the obvious as any human being. He once was the attorney general of the United States, so naturally, he placed the full weight and prestige of his position as the chief law enforcement officer in the country behind the abolitionist cause.

In a slightly hysterical statement before the Senate Judiciary Committee, he enlightened us with a summary of the abolitionists' "moral" argument about the sanctity of human life:

> We live in days of turbulence. Violence is commonplace: murder an hourly occurrence.
>
> In the midst of anxiety and fear, complexity and doubt, perhaps our greatest need is reverence for life—mere life: our lives, the lives of others, all life. Life is an end in itself. A humane and generous concern for every individual, for his safety, his health and his fulfillment, will do more to soothe the savage heart than the fear of state-inflicted death which chiefly serves to remind us how close we are to the jungle.
>
> "Murder and capital punishment are not opposites that cancel one another, but similars that breed their kind," Shaw advises us. When the state itself kills, the mandate "thou shalt not kill" loses the force of the absolute.
>
> Surely the abolition of the death penalty is a major milestone in the long road up from barbarism. There was a time when self-preservation necessitated its imposition. *Later inordinate sacrifices by the innocent would have been required to isolate dangerous persons from the public. Our civilization has no such excuse.*
>
> * * *
>
> Our difficult days call for rare courage: the willingness to disenthrall ourselves, to think and act anew. There is no justification for the death penalty. It cheapens life. Its injustices and inhumanity raise basic questions about our institutions and purpose as a people. Why must we kill? *What do we fear?* What do we accomplish besides our own embitterment? *Why cannot we revere life and in so doing create in the hearts of our people a love for mankind that will finally still violence?*[5] [emphasis supplied]

130

Well, there you have it, the whole thing in a nutshell.

I have emphasized some of the juicier parts of this little manifesto, but first some generalizations. I like the way that Jacques Barzun, the witty historian and writer,* replies to such sweeping moralizations:

> I find the abolitionist inconsistent, narrow or blind. The propaganda for abolition speaks in hushed tones of the sanctity of human life, as if the mere statement of it as an absolute should silence all opponents who have any moral sense.[6]

True enough—as accurate a characterization of the abolitionists' feelings as could be found. Then, with a sort of terrifying logic, Barzun takes their position to its logical (and ridiculous) conclusion:

> Very well: is the movement then campaigning also against the principle of self-defense? Absolute sanctity means letting the cutthroat have his sweet will of you even if you have a poker handy to bash him with, for you might kill.[7]

Neat. Let even the most dedicated abolitionist answer that one and tell us with a straight face that he wouldn't reach for the poker.

Next, in Ramsey Clark's statement we have the usual resounding silence about the plight of the victims of crime. His statement is four pages long** and contains 1342 words. He uses the word "victim" once, *and then only to tell us that executing the murderer won't bring the victim back to life.* It has to be that way, of course; the "sanctity of human life" argument explodes once one points out the selectivity with which the sanctifiers choose the objects of their concern: always the murderers, never the victims.

The parts of Clark's statement that I emphasized when I quoted it deserve some special consideration if we are to try to

*Mr. Barzun was formerly provost of Columbia University and, until his retirement, held the position of University Professor, an honor accorded to no more than three people at one time.
**It was reprinted in *Capital Punishment*, edited by James A. McCafferty, Chicago: Aldine-Atherton (1972).

131

unravel the abolitionists' moral arguments. Clark's prose style runs to the exhortatory. He positively *loves* short, choppy rhetorical questions. To quote him again:

> Why must we kill? What do we fear? What do we accomplish besides our own embitterment?[8]

Charitably viewed, this little run-on indicates that he just got carried away with his own rhetoric; otherwise it's time for the men in the white coats. Ramsey Clark tells us at the beginning of his statement that violence has become commonplace and that murder is an hourly occurrence. Then he asks: "What do we fear?" We can presume that Mr. Clark, as attorney general of the United States, had access to national crime statistics. He made his statement in 1968; during the preceding year there were 12,090 homicides in the United States. 12,000-plus people *died* at the hands of others.

"What do we fear?"

Oh, well. He probably couldn't have used those figures anyway. Somebody might have asked him about the victims.

Now the first statement I emphasized is, to me, a lot more serious. Mr. Clark tells us that "inordinate sacrifices by the innocent" are necessary before we can isolate dangerous persons (presumably by execution since this was the topic under consideration). Then: "Our civilization has no such excuse."

Taking the words "our civilization" to mean the United States on July 2, 1968, the day on which Mr. Clark made the statement, the conclusion is inescapable that he is stating flatly that the 12,090 homicides perpetrated on our citizens in 1967 *did not, in his view, constitute "inordinate sacrifices by the innocent."*

There may be another way to interpret these statements, but it is difficult to imagine. If the above interpretation is correct—12,090 murder victims is *not* an inordinate sacrifice—we have the then attorney general of the United States making one of the most classic antivictim utterances in history, and we are left with the nagging question of just how *many* victims, in Ramsey Clark's view, must die before their "sacrifices" are worthy of our consideration.

132

The foregoing statements by Mr. Clark are scary. The last one emphasized is just ridiculous:

> Why cannot we revere life and in so doing create in the hearts of our people a love of mankind that will finally still violence?[9]

It is doubtful if even Anthony Amsterdam would buy that one. Certainly he has never, to my knowledge, urged on the Supreme Court the thesis that if we revere life (i.e., do not execute murderers), we will create in the hearts of these murderers a "love of mankind," and "finally still violence"—that is, no more killings, armed robberies, rapes, and so on.

Professor Amsterdam probably hasn't used the "love of mankind" bit for two reasons. First, because he couldn't do it with a straight face and levity is unseemly in the highest judicial tribunal in the nation. Second, because, as he well knows, we did start "revering life" from 1968 on by not executing murderers, and violence was not exactly stilled. In fact, homicides rose from 13,650 in that year to 20,075 in 1975, and it would be skating on thin ice to make the "love of mankind" argument if you didn't want to hear about the victims.

The "sanctity of human life" argument is a fairly easy one to deal with, at least from the proponents' point of view. We can concede that it is humane and appealing. *Until*, that is, we interject the victims into the equation, and then we're right back there in Atlanta and Austin and Tallahassee hollering for retention.

The "evolving standards of decency" argument set forth by the abolitionists is more difficult to come to grips with. This is so primarily because nobody can know for sure what the phrase really means. If you accosted 100 people at random on the street and asked them what was meant by "standards of decency," you would probably get a) a punch in the nose, b) a blank stare, or c) as many different answers as there were people willing to respond.

To me, for example, it would be "decent" to execute Richard Speck if only to demonstrate that society places a higher value on the lives of his eight victims than it has done to date.

To Professor Amsterdam it would be "decent" to ensure that we never executed another murderer—neither the commandant of the Buchenwald death camp in World War II Germany, nor a terrorist who wiped out the city of New York with a hydrogen bomb. That is what he told the Supreme Court.[10]

Thus, we really *do* have a definitional problem. Professor Amsterdam used the "evolving standards of decency" argument several times before the Supreme Court in arguing the *Furman* series of cases. He cited a 1958 case, *Trop v. Dulles,*[11] in which the Supreme Court held that it was cruel and unusual punishment under the Eighth Amendment to the Constitution to revoke the United States citizenship of a wartime deserter.

He took a great deal of comfort from the fact that the Court, in deciding *Trop,* said that the Eighth Amendment was to take its meaning "from the evolving standards of decency that mark the progress of a maturing society."[12] The only problem with using *Trop v. Dulles* as a major point of departure was the fact that Chief Justice Warren in that case had expressly warned that the Court was *not* talking about capital punishment as being cruel and unusual punishment "in a day that it was still widely accepted."[13]

That wasn't helpful in the least, but the abolitionists, through Professor Amsterdam, argued that an "evolution" had indeed taken place and that the public no longer supported the death penalty because its collective "standards of decency" had been raised.

This was interesting in view of the fact that the voters of Illinois had retained the death penalty less than two years before, and a 1971 Gallup Poll taken shortly before the case was argued showed that the public favored capital punishment by a margin of 49–40.

So where did Professor Amsterdam dig up his "evolving standards of decency"? Although 40 states had the death penalty on the books, he pointed out, there had been no executions since 1967. The same trend, he added, had led virtually every country in the world to abolish capital punishment.[14] The death penalty was no longer widely accepted.

Two things should be mentioned, however. First, with regard to the contention that other countries were abolishing and therefore *we* should abolish: other countries were not expe-

134

riencing murder epidemics as we were. Canada, for example, which had all but abolished capital punishment in 1965, had 426 murders in 1971.[15] California alone had 1,636 in the same year.[16] Professor Amsterdam was comparing apples and oranges.

Now for the argument that since there had been no executions between 1967 and 1972 (when *Furman* was argued), public support for the death penalty had fallen off. *Of course* there had been no executions. The abolitionists had been doing everything in their power to ensure there would be none.* It was common knowledge in the legal profession that sooner or later the Supreme Court might well rule definitively on the issue and stays of execution were routinely granted.**

At any rate, the "evolving standards" argument convinced Justices Brennan and Marshall in *Furman*. But it didn't get much farther. Justice Stewart took a couple of paragraphs to flatten it in *Gregg v. Georgia*, saying that

> developments during the four years since *Furman* have undercut substantially the assumptions upon which [the "evolving standards" argument] rested.[17]

Finally we come to the argument advanced by the abolitionists that society has no right to be in the retribution business. "Retribution" may be defined concisely as "punishment."

Well, there *is* a school of thought that says we shouldn't punish criminals. Dr. Karl Menninger, in fact, considers it a *crime* to punish them, or even to call them criminals. "Retribution" is a sort of sterile term; the abolitionists prefer words such as

---

*The abolitionists decided in 1968 that "henceforth they would attempt to block all executions"; see Michael Meltsner, *Cruel and Unusual*, New York: Random House (1937), p. 106.

**This brings up a point often raised by the abolitionists. When a convicted criminal, sentenced to death, has exhausted all appeals of his conviction and sentence, together with any other means of delay the abolitionists can devise for him, the claim is then made that the waiting, the delay itself, is "cruel and unusual." This is bootstrapping, pure and simple. Who *caused* the delay?

Effective justice is swift and certain. The way to accomplish this is by providing for speedy trial and an expedited appeal process. For example, Troy Leon Gregg was arrested on November 24, 1973, convicted on February 7, 1974, and his conviction was upheld by the Georgia Supreme Court on October 17, 1974. Less than a year had elapsed.

"vengeance" and "hate," which are intended to conjure up a more harrowing picture.

Victor H. Evjen, former editor of *Federal Probation*, has said about capital punishment:

> The death penalty is more an act of hate and vengeance than it is justice. Retribution cannot be considered a legitimate goal of criminal law. Yet simple retribution is one of the most appealing arguments for the death penalty.
>
> A responsible society wants protection, not revenge. It does not need to avenge itself, nor should it want to do so. Punishment for punishment's sake is not justice and is repugnant to civilized man. The death penalty is not only unnecessary and futile, it is barbaric and brutal.[18]

If it sounds familiar, it should. All of the old catchwords. No mention of the plight of the victims. (Evjen uses the word twice, *to excuse the murderer*: "Most persons involved in homicides do not deliberate on the death of the victim. . .and many do not intend the victim's death.")[19] You read these writers for a while and you are tempted to arrive at the conclusion that it is somehow the fault of the victim that he got murdered.

But, coming back to the concept of retribution, Evjen's most critical statement is that "[society] does not need to avenge itself, nor should it want to do so." That is a crock of nonsense. Society has not only a right but an affirmative duty to punish those who transgress against its members.

But don't take my word for it. Ask somebody who *knew*: Thomas Jefferson, for starters—who wrote:

> Whereas, it frequently happens that wicked and dissolute men, resigning themselves to the dominion of inordinate passions, commit violations on the lives, liberties and property of others, and, the secure enjoyment of these having induced men to enter into society, *government would be defective in its purpose*, were it not to restrain such criminal acts, by inflicting *due punishments* on those who perpetrate them . . .[20] [emphasis supplied]

Thomas Jefferson has established his credentials as a friend of civil liberties by being the architect of the Bill of Rights to the Constitution of the United States (including the Eighth Amendment), and unless we are running into the stone wall of the abolitionist mind-set, his views are more persuasive than those of Victor Evjen.

Ponder the words "government would be defective in its purpose" if it did not punish criminals who prey upon others. Evjen contends the opposite: society has no right to and should not want to. But if this is true, why did we ever "enter into society," as Jefferson phrased it? Obviously for protection from "wicked and dissolute" people, which only society can collectively provide to its members. Certainly we do not wish to return to a system of family states, with each wreaking its individual vengeance upon anyone who injures a member of the clan; but this would assuredly happen were we to cast aside the idea that punishment and retribution have a place in an orderly society.

At any rate, the discussion is academic. The people who count are the ones who set policy for us. First, the legislators in Congress and the several states. Next, the courts that must rule on the constitutionality of those legislators' efforts. Finally, the Supreme Court of the United States.

In the final analysis it was up to the Supreme Court, which held, in *Gregg v. Georgia*, with regard to the question of retribution and the death penalty:

> In part, capital punishment is an expression of society's moral outrage at particularly offensive conduct. This function may be unappealing to many, but it is essential in an ordered society that asks its citizens to rely on legal processes rather than self-help to vindicate their wrongs.[21]

The Court noted that "retribution is no longer the dominant objective of the criminal law."[22] But, it continued,

> neither is it a forbidden objective nor one inconsistent with our respect for the dignity of man [citations omitted].
>
> Indeed the decision that capital punishment may be the appropriate sanction in extreme cases is an expression of the community's belief that certain crimes are themselves so grievous an affront to humanity that the only adequate response may be the penalty of death.[23]

So, retribution or punishment—not, as phrased by the abolitionists in the pejorative manner, "vengeance and hate"—have their place. Apparently society has the constitutional power to protect its own.

The "moral" arguments against capital punishment have a lot going for them. They are enlightened, compassionate, progressive, and they have a certain appeal to everyone. If we were not faced with the fact of 20,000-plus murder victims in this country in the past year, they might be all but unanswerable. But we are; and that is the problem.

Notes

1. Ernest van den Haag, "Death Penalty: A Deterrent...," *Wall Street Journal,* December 3, 1976, p. 20, col. 6.
2. Ira Schwartz, "The Crime of Capital Punishment," *Chicago Tribune,* December 5, 1976, sec. 2, p. 1, col. 4.
3. Van den Haag, *op. cit.*
4. A very helpful book is *Capital Punishment,* edited by James A. McCafferty, Chicago: Aldine-Atherton (1972).
5. Statement by Attorney General Ramsey Clark before the Subcommittee on Criminal Laws and Procedures of the Senate Judiciary Committee on S. 1760 to Abolish the Death Penalty, July 2, 1968.
6. Jacques Barzun, "In Favor of Capital Punishment," *The American Scholar,* vol. 31, no. 2, Spring 1962.
7. *Ibid.*
8. Clark, *op. cit.,* note 5.
9. *Ibid.*
10. Summary of Oral Argument, *Woodson v. North Carolina, Criminal Law Reporter,* April 7, 1976, vol. 19, p. 4010.
11. 386 U.S. 86 (1958).
12. *Ibid.,* at page 101.
13. *Ibid.,* at page 99.
14. *Woodson v. North Carolina, op. cit.,* note 10, p. 4148.
15. George P. Brimmel, "Death Penalty," *National Observer,* January 13, 1973, p. 7, col. 1.
16. Unpublished flier of the California Peace Officers Association, available from the author.
17. 96 S. Ct. 2909, at page 2928 (1976).
18. Victor H. Evjen, "Let's Abolish Capital Punishment," reprinted in McCafferty, *op. cit.,* note 4, p. 223.
19. *Ibid.,* p. 220.
20. Thomas Jefferson, "A Bill for Proportioning Crimes and Punishments, in cases heretofore Capital," *The Writings of Thomas Jefferson,* issued under the auspices of the Thomas Jefferson Memo-

rial Association of the United States, Washington, D.C. (1905), vol. 1, p. 218.

21. 96 S. Ct. 2909, at page 2915 (1976), footnote omitted.
22. *Ibid.*; citing *Williams v. New York,* 337 U.S. 241, at page 248 (1949).
23. *Ibid.*

Part III

THE SUPREME ARBITER: THE SUPREME COURT AND THE DEATH PENALTY

CHAPTER 9

Overview

We turn now to the ten-year (1967–1976) seesaw battle over capital punishment that raged in the tribunal that has the final say in such matters: the Supreme Court of the United States. That Court has, quite literally, the power of life and death over the *entire* death-row population in this country, because only the Court has power under our Constitution to strike down or to uphold death penalty laws throughout the country.

It proved that it was perfectly willing to exercise this power in the two series of landmark cases: *Furman v. Georgia*, which struck down capital punishment as applied in 1972; and *Gregg v. Georgia*, which upheld the death penalty generally and certain specific statutes providing for its application in 1976.

A word here about nomenclature. I will attempt to tell the story in as nontechnical and nonlegalistic a manner as is possible. As noted in the introduction, this book is not meant to be a legal treatise. We are, however, talking about the law, at its highest level; and, of necessity, some legal terminology must come into play.

143

First, the names of the cases. When the Supreme Court decides to hear a series of cases in order to get wider input on singularly important issues, it generally consolidates them so as to receive briefs and hear oral arguments on all of the cases taken as a whole. Then, when the Court announces its decision on the series of cases, it usually selects one of them as a lead-off case in which it announces the general principles of law applicable to all, writing separate opinions in the others in order to clarify distinctions of fact and law.

The individual defendant who is lucky (or unlucky) enough to have his case selected as the lead-off case becomes, by a sort of shorthand, a household word in the legal profession, and, if the issue is of sufficient notoriety or importance, in the nation.

Thus the late Ernesto Miranda achieved world-wide fame because the Court chose him as the lead-off man in its series of cases that revolutionized (for better or worse) the law on police interrogations and confessions by criminal suspects.*

By the same token, one William Henry Furman, convicted for murder in the course of a burglary, skyrocketed to enduring legal, and perhaps national, fame when the Court used the case of *Furman v. Georgia* as the main case in that particular series. "Furman" is now the universal term that symbolizes the greatest victory the abolitionists ever won, perhaps ever will win.

In legal circles, especially in the somewhat close-knit world of capital punishment advocates (on either side), the names of Furman's companions at the bar, Earnest James Aikens, Jr. (vs. California), Lucious Jackson (vs. Georgia), and Elmer Branch (vs. Texas) are of co-equal, or almost co-equal, importance; but it is William Henry Furman who, besides having his life spared, became a part of legal history.

Troy Leon Gregg, convicted of a double robbery-murder in Georgia, got the lead-off nod in the series of cases in 1976,** but

---

*Miranda himself, whose rape conviction was reversed by the Supreme Court, was retried, convicted, and sent to prison; he was finally paroled, broke parole, was returned inside, and after his re-release liked to go around selling autographed copies of police *Miranda* warning cards. He was stabbed to death in a Phoenix bar in 1975. The story goes that the man suspected of killing him invoked his right to remain silent under the *Miranda* decision and had to be released.

**Gregg's companions before the court were Charles William Proffitt (vs. Florida), Jerry Lane Jurek (vs. Texas), James Tyrone Woodson (vs. North Carolina), and Stanislaus Roberts (vs. Louisiana).

his fame may be posthumous. This time the Court, while striking the mandatory death penalty statutes of Louisiana and North Carolina, upheld Gregg's conviction and death sentence, the Georgia statute, and capital punishment generally. "Gregg" is now the shorthand term for the proponents' greatest victory.

In discussing the cases, the same shorthand expressions will be used—one name representing the series except when there are differing questions of fact and law.

Another term that will see a lot of action is *amicus curiae*, Latin for "friend of the court." In cases as important as *Furman* and *Gregg*, other parties want to be heard. They believe that the issues transcend the actual litigants themselves—a given defendant and a given state—so they petition the Court for leave to enter the case as *amicus curiae*, either by filing a brief or by participating in oral argument. Basically, such a petitioner represents to the court that it has special expertise in the issue under consideration and that it can produce novel and different arguments, generally of an empirical and/or philosophical nature to buttress the cause of the party that it is supporting.

If the court believes that the petitioner does indeed possess such expertise, it usually grants a motion to file a brief as *amicus curiae* and receives the brief. Permission to participate in oral argument is very rarely granted. Petitioners must be responsible entities; *amicus curiae* advocacy from fringe groups of the right or the left is not welcomed.

Amicus curiae, or its plural, *amici curiae*, when two or more entities join in the same brief, perform two important functions. The mere request for permission to file immediately highlights for the Court the importance attached to the issue before it in legal, and often political and sociological, circles (although this was hardly necessary in *Furman* and *Gregg*). Additionally, *amicus curiae* advocacy has been useful in presenting to the Court additional arguments that are helpful to it in reaching its decision.

This author has filed some 20 briefs on criminal-justice issues before the Supreme Court on behalf of Americans for Effective Law Enforcement, Inc.,* and served as co-counsel in

*Americans for Effective Law Enforcement, Inc. (AELE) is a national, not-for-profit citizens organization dedicated to representing the rights of the law-abiding and the victims of crime. This author is AELE's executive director (AELE, 960 State National Bank Plaza, Evanston, Illinois 60201).

oral argument once. A cardinal rule of *amicus* advocacy is: Don't file unless you have arguments to put forth *in addition* to those made by the party you are supporting. Never simply repeat what has already been said in the brief-in-chief. The justices are busy men and they don't want to read the same thing twice. Brevity is also important; an *amicus* "brief" should be just that. Some of the most spectacular work done in *Furman* and *Gregg* was done by *amicus curiae*, as will be discussed shortly.

1968 was a watershed year in the capital punishment controversy. To begin with, it was the first year in recent history in which no executions took place in the United States. This was no accident. The Legal Defense Fund of the National Association for the Advancement of Colored People made a calculated decision to use a major part of its considerable talents and resources to bring about a total moratorium on executions.

Michael Meltsner, a Fund attorney, describes the strategy:

> Abolition needed a symbol, a threat of crisis, to overcome inertia and to win favor from a reluctant judiciary.
> One way to promote this end was to raise the entire range of capital punishment arguments in all cases where execution was imminent, thereby stopping the killing and eventually presenting any resumption of it as likely to lead to a blood bath.[1]

The Fund attorneys accomplished this with consummate skill. Pending before the Supreme Court was the case of *Maxwell v. Bishop*, Number 622 on the calendar of the Court's October 1968 term. *Maxwell* involved an Arkansas rapist, convicted and sentenced to die. NAACP Legal Defense Fund attorneys contended that Maxwell, a black man convicted of raping a white woman, had received the death penalty solely because of race. This was an important issue and the Court's decision could have the greatest possible impact upon the capital punishment issue nationwide.

As Meltsner phrases it:

> It was now 1968, however, and several intervening developments had made it far more attractive for the Supreme Court to confront the constitutionality of capital

case procedure. Prodded perhaps by a growing awareness that LDF had halted executions across the nation, the Court itself had contributed to legal developments which made the decision of large questions inevitable.[2]

They got their moratorium. One must admire success, and they were successful beyond question. No one was executed between 1968, when the moratorium strategy began, and 1972, when *Furman* was argued, due in large measure to the tactics of the LDF.

Along with their moratorium, the abolitionists got something they hadn't bargained for. The lid was put on in 1967, and there were 12,090 criminal homicides that year. By 1976, when *Gregg* was argued, the murder count had climbed to more than 20,000. No executions and the number of homicides shot up 40 percent in eight years. Any correlation between the two facts was, of course, purely coincidental to the abolitionist; but to the man in the street (who votes for his state legislators, who in turn vote for capital punishment) the correlation was there. Why else would public sentiment in favor of executing murderers harden, as it undeniably did during the years of the moratorium that the LDF and others had worked so long and hard to achieve?

We need look only briefly at what the Supreme Court had done with the "cruel and unusual punishment" clause of the Eighth Amendment prior to 1968. It had, to be sure, applied the clause to protect citizens' rights in several cases not involving the death penalty. For example, in 1910 the Court had before it the case of a poor wretch named Weems who had defrauded the Coast Guard of 612 pesos in Manila at the time the Philippine Islands were a U.S. mandate.[3] The Court had to decide whether a sentence of 15 years at hard labor, chained ankle and wrist, with a loss of all civil rights forever, might not be cruel and unusual—disproportionate to the offense. It was, said the Court (over the dissents of Justices Edward D. White and Oliver Wendell Holmes). The Eighth Amendment prohibited that sort of thing.

Trop v. Dulles[4] held, in 1958, that loss of citizenship for a wartime deserter was cruel and unusual punishment. That was the case in which the "evolving standards of decency" lan-

147

guage that so intrigued the abolitionists was first used, although the language was accompanied by an admonition by Chief Justice Warren that capital punishment itself was still not "cruel and unusual."

In 1962 the Court put a new wrinkle into the Eighth Amendment when it held that California could not punish someone simply for *being* a narcotics addict; it could punish him for possession of narcotics or sale of narcotics, but punishment for the mere status of addiction violated the Eighth Amendment.

That case, *Robinson v. California*,[5] did hold out one glimmer of hope for the long-range abolitionist strategy. The Court held that the protections of the Bill of Rights to the federal Constitution, the Eighth Amendment in particular, were applicable to the citizens of the several states through the Fourteenth Amendment, and that states could not pass laws that infringed upon rights guaranteed by the federal Constitution.

But in none of these cases was the central issue that of capital punishment. To the contrary, the Court had held, down through the decades, that the death penalty was recognized as an appropriate criminal sanction by the framers of the Constitution and that it was not cruel and unusual under the Eighth Amendment unless it was inflicted in a way that was barbarous, involved torture or a lingering death, or caused something more than "the necessary suffering involved in any method employed to extinguish life humanely."[6]

The argument that capital punishment was cruel and unusual per se was rejected as far back as 1878, when the Court upheld Utah's method of execution by public shooting.[7] In 1890 electrocution was okayed,[8] and in 1947 the justices refused to find anything cruel and unusual in a *second* execution after the first one had failed.[9]

Then along came Earl Warren, as late as 1958 in *Trop v. Dulles*, and told everybody, without really being asked to, that the death penalty was *still* constitutional.[10]

This was a pretty heavy line of precedent for the LDF and their colleagues to face if they meant to cut through all the underbrush and knock off capital punishment forever at the highest judicial level in the nation. But they were men worthy of the task; they rolled up their sleeves and got on with the job.

Notes

1. Michael Meltsner, *Cruel and Unusual*, New York: Random House (1973), p. 107.
2. *Ibid.*
3. *Weems v. United States*, 217 U.S. 349 (1910).
4. 356 U.S. 86 (1958).
5. 370 U.S. 660 (1962).
6. *Francis v. Resweber*, 329 U.S. 459 (1947), at page 464.
7. *Wilkerson v. Utah*, 99 U.S. 130 (1878).
8. *In re Kemmler*, 136 U.S. 436 (1890).
9. *Francis v. Resweber*, 329 U.S. 459 (1947).
10. *Trop v. Dulles, supra*, n. 4.

CHAPTER 10

The Preliminary Skirmishes

The abolitionists were riding high by the spring of 1969. Their moratorium was a complete success: nobody had been executed in the United States since July 1967, and the little clouds just beginning to gather on the horizon, which would soon become a thunderstorm of angry public reaction to soaring homicide rates, were scarcely noticeable.

Moreover, the Court seemed to be getting its act together as far as the LDF and other foes of capital punishment were concerned. Two important cases had been decided in 1968 that clearly signaled that if the Court was perhaps unready to overturn the death penalty altogether, it was at least going to scrutinize such cases through a *very* fine eyepiece.

In the throes of a national reaction to, and revulsion over, the kidnapping and murder of the baby of Charles Lindbergh (who was at the time not so much a national hero as a sort of walking national shrine), Congress in 1934 enacted the "Little Lindbergh Law," which provided a federal death penalty for any kidnapping in which the victim suffered physical harm.

150

The statute provided, however, that the death penalty was *only* applicable if the accused was found guilty by a jury. If he pleaded guilty or was convicted by a judge sitting without a jury, the maximum sentence would be life imprisonment.

In the case of *Jackson v. United States,*[1] the court ruled that this provision was unconstitutional because the threat of death *might* coerce, and certainly would *encourage,* a guilty plea, thus deterring and discouraging the exercise of the constitutional right of a trial by jury.

The Court struck the death penalty provisions out of the "Little Lindbergh Law" (and by inference from all federal and state laws with similar penalty provisions). The abolitionists were quick to take advantage of this.

Michael Meltsner described the feelings of the LDF attorneys after *Jackson:*

> The Supreme Court had not merely demonstrated a willingness to tackle a murky question of capital case procedures, but had answered the question in a way which permitted abolitionists to challenge the practices of states with similar defects in their laws.[2]

The Court did not overturn the laws entirely, and all *convictions* remained in effect; but no one could be *executed* under the laws, which pleased the abolitionists hugely. It was a step in the right direction as far as they were concerned.

And if, incidentally, the *Jackson* decision freed from the threat of execution one Duane Pope, a college lad who, wearying of his studies, had robbed a Nebraska bank and brutally murdered several people,[3] that just had to be. Oh, some people might get upset, but who cares about public opinion, and anyway, it wouldn't bring his victims back to life.

Significantly, Justice Potter Stewart, writing for the six-man majority in *Jackson,* made his first tentative appearance as the single most important justice on the Court in capital punishment issues.

The abolitionists got another shot in the arm in 1968 when the Court decided *Witherspoon v. Illinois.*[4] William Witherspoon was convicted in 1960 of the murder of a Chicago policeman. He was sentenced to death. At his trial, prospective jurors who had scruples against, or objected to, the death penalty were routinely excluded, a practice employed by most states in selecting juries for capital trials. This practice the Court found unconstitutional on the general grounds that it would result in "hanging juries."

The Court left *some* leeway for the state. If a prospective juror said that he would *never* vote for death under any circumstances, he could still be excluded; but if he merely objected to capital punishment on general principles he could not be excluded, at least not routinely.

Potter Stewart again wrote for the 6–3 majority of the Court. The late Justice Hugo Black, in his dissenting opinion, testily told the majority:

> If this Court is to hold capital punishment unconstitutional, I think it should do so forthrightly, not by making it impossible for states to get juries that will enforce the death penalty.[5]

A lot of people thought, and the abolitionists certainly hoped, that *Witherspoon* would effectively overturn the death penalty because the numerical chances of getting someone opposed to capital punishment on a jury had now dramatically increased.

But it didn't work out that way. I'm not sure why, nor have I seen any literature explaining exactly why, juries continued to hand down sentences of death. But one theory is worth exploring. *Witherspoon* is, of course, only valuable to a capital defendant as long as there are people who have reservations about the death penalty. The abolitionists' moratorium was still in effect, *and* homicides were increasing, *and* public opinion was continuing to harden. It just may be that there were fewer and fewer people who objected to capital punishment.

The Supreme Court made the *Witherspoon* decision retroactive. Any person sentenced to death by a jury from which jurors who had scruples against the death penalty had been excluded could now claim that his sentence was unconstitutional. The LDF got busy with *that* little number as fast as they could and they saved any number of persons from execution. (The convictions still stood.)

One beneficiary of the *Witherspoon* decision was Richard Franklin Speck. Back in 1966 when he killed all the nurses, mass murder was not the fairly common phenomenon that it is now, and Chicago has never been famous as a bastion of liberalism or tolerance, particularly for murderers. The Second City has always taken a sort of grisly pride in the number of *gangland* murders committed within its confines, but regular murders are another ball game, and Richard Speck's crime had, at the time, horrified people as no murder had before.

Witherspoon packed a double whammy in Chicago: the killer of a Chicago policeman had been *directly* spared and Speck had almost assuredly been spared, indirectly, from the electric chair. This happy combination (from the abolitionist point of view) just might, though I'll never be able to prove it, have had some effect on the two-to-one vote in 1970 to retain the death penalty in Illinois.

Those little clouds of public opinion were still gathering on the horizon. There were a few ominous rumbles of thunder. But the abolitionists, delighted with their victories, could not have been expected to notice.

1969 had started well for the abolitionists but it turned out not to be a vintage year. They had pinned great hopes on a case called *Maxwell v. Bishop,* which the Court in 1968 had agreed to review.[6] It was an appealing case from the abolitionist point of view and not one, on the facts, that the proponents would want to pursue.

William Maxwell, a black man, had been convicted of raping a white woman and sentenced to die by a jury. It was a "single verdict" case, that is, the jury heard the evidence and then decided whether to convict or not, and what the punishment should be, in one verdict. Under the single-verdict system, the jury had no way of hearing about other circumstances that might tend to mitigate the heinousness of the crime and so mitigate the sentence.

In addition, the defense had a wealth of statistics, compiled by the respected criminologist Marvin Wolfgang of the University of Pennsylvania, suggesting that blacks who raped white women were much more likely to get the death sentence than other rapists. Was this due to racial discrimination? If so, the penalty should be declared cruel and unusual under the Eighth Amendment. This would be one of the harder cases for the proponents to meet, and the abolitionists hoped it would free hundreds from the sentence of death.*

Argument was heard in *Maxwell v. Bishop* on March 4, 1969. The defense team thought that they had the votes and were *really* going to make some law. If the single verdict and racial issues were resolved in their favor and, as expected, the decision was made retroactive like *Witherspoon* and *Jackson*, the exodus from death row would look like people lined up to get out of the stadium after a Super Bowl game.

Then all hell broke loose in the Supreme Court itself. Justice Abe Fortas, a brilliant liberal jurist whose vote had been counted to go in Maxwell's favor, resigned on May 14, 1969 under the pressure of some conflict of interest charges; and on May 26 the Court ordered reargument of *Maxwell v. Bishop* at a later date.

Another thing disturbed the abolitionists. During the first argument, Justice Potter Stewart had asked Professor Amsterdam, who argued for Maxwell, if *Witherspoon* did not apply to the case: if jurors with scruples against the death penalty had been excluded from his trial, then Maxwell's death sentence would have to be reversed on that ground and the Court need not reach the single verdict/racial discrimination argument.

The Supreme Court has an unwritten rule: if a case can be decided on an already established principle of law, it will be. The Court will not break *new* ground unless the issue is squarely before it and no alternative grounds of decision appear.

Here was the irony of ironies. The abolitionists had positively rejoiced over the *Witherspoon* decision. But now they *wanted* the Court to come to grips with what they properly considered to be *very strong* arguments against the single verdict, whereby the jury decides on a penalty without benefit of additional information, and against capital punishment for rape— the racial discrimination argument.

But Potter Stewart, who won abolitionist accolades for writ-

*They had another case, *Boykin v. Alabama,* which involved a death sentence for armed robbery, but the issue was never reached. Boykin's guilty plea was vacated on other grounds, namely whether it was voluntarily entered or not; 395 U.S. 6 (1969).

ing *Witherspoon*, was now talking about turning it around and mooting out the best case that had come down the pike in a long time.

And then there was William Maxwell to consider. He had been on death row for a long time and probably did not want to play the part of a Nathan Hale for the abolitionist cause. If *Witherspoon* would get him off death row, that was all right by him! Worry about other theories later.

Well, that is how it happened, anyway. The case was reargued and on June 1, 1970 it was disposed of—based on *Witherspoon*. The Court sent it back to the lower federal courts to see if it should be reversed on jury-selection grounds. The LDF attorneys who had nurtured the case like a tender blossom for years, because the issues were so *right* for their cause, must have felt a pang of disappointment, like actors suddenly deprived of an important role in a play.

But William Maxwell probably packed his belongings and moved off death row (he *wasn't* freed) with a considerable sense of relief.

1970 and 1971 brought more disappointments for the abolitionists.

Jackson and *Witherspoon* had been unmitigated victories, except insofar as *Witherspoon* had spoiled the potential of *Maxwell v. Bishop* to break capital punishment for good.

Now along came two unappealing people whom the Court decided to hear about in its efforts to resolve the controversy. (That was *one* bright spot—the Justices hadn't lost interest.) Dennis McGautha, with a long prior record of criminal convictions, had been convicted of robbery-murder in California and sentenced to death. James Crampton, an Ohio narcotics addict, had the unusual distinction of presenting what was probably the first case to reach the Supreme Court involving someone who murdered his victim (his wife) as she sat on the toilet. His sentence was death.

Both McGautha and Crampton never denied their guilt. Each claimed that if juries had no standards for sentencing, the opportunity for caprice and mistake rendered the entire process unconstitutional. California had a process for determining guilt

155

at one stage of the trial and the penalty at another. Ohio didn't, so Crampton threw in the "single verdict" argument that had not been reached in *Maxwell v. Bishop.*

McGautha and Crampton both lost.[7] A majority of the Court, on May 3, 1971, found no constitutional defects in the process by which either of them had been sentenced to death: standardless jury discretion, single verdicts, and so on. And it refused to hold capital punishment unconstitutional *per se.*

The cases were so sordid, the defendants so dismal. Perhaps that is one of the reasons that they will be almost footnote cases in the legal wrangles over capital punishment. Even the LDF couldn't work up enough interest to do anything more than file an *amicus curiae* brief. Tony Amsterdam stayed in California; Fund attorneys attended the oral argument only as observers.[8]

To anyone else but abolitionists, *McGautha* and *Crampton* would have set seal on the matter. To anyone else but United States Marines, the Japanese resistance to the landing at Tarawa would have called for "retreat and regrouping." There is a certain similarity: the tough tenaciousness of those who *know* they are in the right and are going to get the job accomplished.

There *was* a certain amount of regrouping among the LDF forces right after *McGautha-Crampton* came down. On May 15 and 16, an emergency conference was called at Columbia University Law School to decide what to do. The consensus was "Retreat, hell!" again to paraphrase the Marines. They were going ahead. Last-ditch strategy was planned.

Then on June 28 a beachhead was opened, roughly equivalent to the seizure of the first intact Rhine River bridge at Remagen during the Allied advance across Germany during the last days of World War II. The Court, on June 28, 1971, granted review of the cases of William Henry Furman, Earnest Aikens, Jr., Lucious Jackson, and Elmer Branch.

> The question to be resolved was: Does the imposition and carrying out of the death penalty in this case constitute cruel and unusual punishment in violation of the Eighth and Fourteenth Amendments [to the Constitution of the United States]?[9]

Finally. An initial victory of unprecedented proportions. They had *the* question before the Court. Now they had to win the case and they geared up to do just that. The rumblings of the public opinion storm clouds were more audible than ever, but in their elation the abolitionists took no notice.

Notes

1. 390 U.S. 570 (1968).
2. Michael Meltsner, *Cruel and Unusual*, New York: Random House (1973), p. 118.
3. *Pope v. United States*, 392 U.S. 651 (1968).
4. 391 U.S. 510 (1968).
5. 491 U.S. 510 at page 532.
6. 393 U.S. 997 (1968).
7. *McGautha v. California; Crampton v. Ohio*, 402 U.S. 183 (1971).
8. Meltsner, *op. cit.*, p. 229.
9. 403 U.S. 952 (1971).

CHAPTER 11

Furman v. Georgia:
Winning the Battle

William Henry Furman is the living embodiment of why someone years ago thought up the felony-murder rule: If you are committing a felony and someone is killed in the process, you are guilty of capital murder. Period.

Furman had entered the Georgia home of 29-year-old William Joseph Micke, Jr., for the purpose of committing a felony—burglary. He was armed. Mr. Micke went downstairs to investigate. Furman ran out and, in the process, tripped; his gun discharged through a door, killing Mr. Micke. Furman was convicted of felony-murder and sentenced to death.[1]

Earnest James Aikens, Jr., of California, had been sentenced to death for raping and stabbing to death Mrs. Mary Winifred Eaton. He had also been convicted of the same crime against Mrs. Kathleen Neil Dodd, the pregnant mother of two children. The state of California introduced evidence at his trial that he had committed a third murder and a rape in 1962.[2]

Lucious Jackson, a black man, had escaped from a Georgia prison gang and forcibly raped a 21-year-old white woman. He was convicted of the crime and sentenced to death.[3]

Elmer Branch, black, 20 years old, with an IQ of 67, received the death penalty in Texas for the forcible rape and robbery of a 65-year-old white woman.[4]

These were the LDF's immediate clients in what could well be a landmark case. None of them could be called *good* men by any stretch of the imagination, but with the exception of Earnest James Aikens, Jr. (who, ironically, would be spared before *Furman* was even decided, a beneficiary of the California Supreme Court's decision to outlaw capital punishment in that state in February of 1972), none filled the public with more than the usual repugnance.

And, again with the exception of Aikens, the crimes for which they had been sentenced to death—particularly Jackson's and Branch's, which did not result in the death of their victims—provided excellent fodder for the abolitionists' argument that the penalty was applied in an arbitrary and discriminatory manner.

Theoretically, the Supreme Court decides cases strictly upon its interpretation of the Constitution of the United States. The depravity of the defendants should not be a factor in their deliberations and I am certain that the justices make every effort to purge their minds of such considerations. But they are human beings, not computers. The abolitionists could be reasonably pleased with the batch of cases that the Court had decided to review.

At least they would not have to plead for the sanctity of human life when the Court came in fresh from reading the facts of the crimes committed by Lance and Kelbach, Speck, and Charlie Manson.

The Legal Defense Fund attorneys were nothing if not professional and thorough in preparing their case. LDF attorney Michael Meltsner, in his book *Cruel and Unusual*,[5] reprinted a memorandum from Professor Amsterdam, who argued two of the cases, to the LDF staffers. He knew what he wanted:

(1) Hugo Bedau has agreed to send JH [Himmelstein] within 10 days:
    (a) a 10-page review of the sociological literature on deterrence, with references.
    (b) a 10-page memo on the world history of capital punishment, focusing on ... the progressive abandonment of the death penalty ...;

(c) a brief memo on the role of scientists and learned men in that history, stressing the enlightened character of abolitionists;

(d) some notes on humanistic literature . . .

JH will ask Hugo if he can expand (b) to include an intellectual history of the struggle about capital punishment; identifying the arguments made for and against it at various stages, and the identities of the makers.

(2) [We must] . . . design an economic cost analysis of the administration of capital punishment.

(3) As per my discussion with Doug Lyons on 7/22, DL is doing

(a) a memo on published descriptions of executions;*

(b) some notes on humanistic literature to add his reflections to [Bedau's] in point (1) (d) *supra*.

(4) The following memos will be assigned within the LDF office:

(a) . . . the major conceptual approach to an argument that the Eighth Amendment is concerned with the psychiatric state of the man who undergoes a punishment: i.e., that a punishment which might constitutionally be applied to A may be unconstitutionally cruel and unusual punishment as applied to B; and, specifically, that it violates the Eighth Amendment to kill persons of diminished mental capacity . . .

(b) . . . recent Eighth Amendment developments in noncapital cases in the lower courts, with emphasis on the themes of (i) evolving character of Eighth Amendment invalidations of penal practices that were widely accepted in 1791; and (ii) the nature of the tests applied to determine whether a penalty is cruel and unusual.

(c) . . . (i) An exhaustive review of [Supreme Court] Eighth Amendment decisions, involving two parts: (A) analyses of each case, including the issues; the holding; the language used to define the Eighth Amendment test, standard or approach employed to judge the constitutionality of penalties challenged as cruel and unusual; and any references made by the Court to interpretative aids (constitutional history, English history, world history, etc.);

*Note: I am not clear whether Doug's memo (a) will include descriptions of the psychological sufferings of men on death row awaiting execution, as well as gory execution scenes. . .

and (B) analyses of the support which the cases lend to [the following theories] (1) the Eighth Amendment standard is dynamic, not static; it evolves, and may condemn in 1971 what it permitted in 1791; (2) rarity of application of a penalty is a major (or at least a relevant) consideration in branding it cruel and unusual; (3) enlightened conceptions of "decency" and "human dignity" are the measure of the Amendment; (4) judges look to enlightened contemporary moral standards, with some independence of legislative judgment, in applying the Eighth Amendment to test legislation; (5) punishment which is disproportionately severe is unconstitutional under the Eighth Amendment, so that a penalty which might be constitutional for crime A may be cruel and unusual for crime B; and, in particular, death is disproportionately severe for rape; (6) punishment which is "unnecessarily" harsh violates the Eighth Amendment, so that courts must consider whether lesser penalties would not equally serve the end supposed to justify a harsher one; (7) the psychiatric state of the person upon whom a punishment is imposed is relevant . . . ; and (8) mental suffering, as well as physical suffering, is relevant. . .

(d) . . . A history of the punishments in common use in the Colonies, England and other "civilized" nations in 1791, to show that banishment, dismemberment, flogging, stocking, branding, etc., were widespread, for the purpose of demonstrating that the death penalty cannot be sustained in 1971 upon the theory that it was commonly used at the time of adoption of the Eighth Amendment without also asserting that these horrors are all equally constitutional. (Also it might be useful to have a separate, brief memo demonstrating that *public* executions were the order of the day in 1791, and that our present unobvious executions are a product of a later era.)

The one thing that is not covered in this list which is a high priority item is a memorandum on the rarity of death sentences and of executions in the twentieth century . . . How about this one, Jack?[6]

They weren't going to miss any bets. They planned to use every argument imaginable to defeat the death penalty once and for all: lack of deterrence, historical arguments, humanistic arguments, the horror of executions, economic cost factors, arbitrariness, discrimination, the "moral" arguments (see Chapter 8), and whatever legal arguments they could bring to bear.

In most cases, when an attorney files a brief in an appellate court he concentrates on the law. That is what appeals courts are for: to interpret the *law*. But the law was not on Tony Amsterdam's side. After all, hadn't the Court just said in *McGautha* and *Crampton* that it was highly unlikely, in its view, that capital punishment would be declared *per se* unconstitutional? He must win his case *in spite of* the law.

The abolitionists of the LDF had plenty of help. Lawyers, law students, and consultants from across the nation, perhaps sensing victory, funneled in their assistance. *Amicus curiae* briefs supporting the defendants (who are referred to as "petitioners" in Supreme Court parlance, since they originally asked for review of their cases—the other side are the "respondents") fluttered down like confetti upon the Supreme Court from:

- A group of governors and ex-governors of nine states.
- Six correctional administrators and prison wardens.
- An Ad Hoc Committee of Psychiatrists for Evaluation of the Death Penalty.
- The Synagogue Council of America.
- Fourteen religious denominational councils or groups.
- A group representing the major religious councils of the state of West Virginia (an abolition state).
- The NAACP, National Urban League, Southern Christian Leadership Conference, Mexican-American Legal Defense and Educational Fund, and the National Council of Negro Women.
- The National Legal Aid and Defender Association.
- The American Civil Liberties Union.
- The State of Alaska.[7]

Pretty heavy stuff.

Arrayed against this laundry list of *amici* who represented almost everybody under the sun (except, of course, the victims) were the attorneys general of the states of Texas, Georgia, and California (or their assistants designated to argue the case), who by law represent their respective states in the Supreme Court.

Theodore Sendak, the articulate attorney general of the state of Indiana, whose hard-line law-and-order stance had made him the greatest single votegetter in the history of that state (and a man to watch in the future on the national political scene), filed a brief as *amicus curiae* in support of the respondents.

The states presented the time-tested arguments, legal and empirical, that had kept capital punishment as a major factor in the criminal jurisprudence of the United States from our country's birth. They said:

- The framers of the Constitution clearly believed that capital punishment was an acceptable means of protecting society from those "wicked and dissolute men" (and women) that Thomas Jefferson liked to talk about.
- Supreme Court decisions, from *Wilkerson v. Utah* in 1878 to *McGautha* and *Crampton* in 1971, had never questioned, on a constitutional basis, the validity of the penalty.
- Capital punishment and its retention or abolition were principally the province of the Congress and the state legislatures.
- "Evolving standards of decency" did not render the punishment unconstitutional, and, acknowledging the trend towards limiting the *application* of the penalty, this did not mean that it was unacceptable to society.
- Retribution was a legitimate end in any system of justice.
- The death penalty deterred would-be murderers.
- There was nothing arbitrary or discriminatory in the application of the death penalty.[8]

The stage was now set. The curtain went up on Monday, January 17, 1972.

The clerk of the Supreme Court issues to counsel appearing before the Court a helpful little card that tells them how to start off their argument ("Mr. Chief Justice, and may it please the Court"), and gives a seating chart identifying each justice and where he sits on the bench: the chief justice and then each associate justice in descending order of seniority, alternating from the right to the left of the chief justice out towards the end of the bench. The card read, on that date:

<pre>
                    BURGER
        DOUGLAS   BRENNAN
        STEWART   WHITE
        MARSHALL   BLACKMUN
POWELL   REHNQUIST
</pre>

Any advocate before the Court is a fool if he needs his little
card. He should know each justice on sight, should have studied all of the Court's prior opinions on the subject, and generally, should be able to say what the justices like for breakfast.
They sit there embodying all of the majesty of the supreme de-
liberative body of the greatest nation in the world, but they are
also human beings, each with his own philosophy, and counsel
should know each justice and his philosophy by heart. That is
how cases are won.

The lineup of counsel on that momentous day:

- For Aikens (California) and Furman (Georgia): Professor
  Anthony Amsterdam. *Murder charges.*
- For Jackson (Georgia): Jack Greenberg of the Legal De-
  fense Fund. *Rape charge.*
- For Branch (Texas): Melvin Carson Bruder of Dallas.
  Rape charge.
- For the state of California: Ronald M. George of the attor-
  ney general's office.
- For the State of Georgia: Mrs. Dorothy Beasley of the at-
  torney general's office.
- For the state of Texas: Professor Charles Alan Wright of
  the University of Texas Law School, representing the of-
  fice of the attorney general.

The first and great commandment in arguing before the Supreme Court is "thou shalt watch thy lights": two little lights
on the lectern—white, you have five more minutes; red, stop
in mid-sentence (unless, of course, a justice is asking you a
question, then you can go on as long as you wish, provided you
can keep the colloquy going). Each side is generally allotted 30
minutes to argue its case, and the side leading off is permitted
to reserve a few minutes of its time for rebuttal of what the opposing side has had to say. Time limits are rigidly adhered to,
unless, as noted above, counsel is responding to a justice when
the red light goes on; otherwise, shut up and sit down.

There is only one way to prepare for oral argument: know

every detail of your case and be prepared to answer any question about it that the justices might throw at you. (One horrible example of lack of preparation that I witnessed: Mr. Justice Stevens, who was appointed in 1975 by President Ford, asked counsel a question to the effect: "I think that the case of *So-and-So v. So-and-So* completely supports your position, wouldn't you agree?" Counsel: "Uh ... well, I really don't know about that case." Scratch one vote.)

Some Supreme Court advocates write out their entire argument and read it to the Court. Some memorize their argument— all 30 minutes of it. Others go up with a very carefully prepared outline: case law, empirical arguments, etc., laid out where they can get to it.

Some pitiful few choose to "wing it." They give a cursory glance at their written brief and then step up to the lectern, ready to argue *ad hoc*. There are a few pathetic corpses of such attorneys scattered about the landscape of the legal profession's gossip: "Did you hear what Justice Rehnquist did to So-and-So?"

The preparation had better be, and usually is, meticulous, even though counsel knows that he may get no more than an opening paragraph out of his mouth before he is hit with the first question from the bench, and he will be lucky if he gets to return to his prepared argument in the next 30 minutes.

But that is what oral argument is really all about. The justices must make decisions that may well affect every citizen in this country and they have certain questions in their own minds that they want answered after they have read the written briefs of the parties and *amici curiae* (if any). The right answers to these questions have been known to win cases.

It is a serious business. The justices may, on occasion, appear to be playing ducks and drakes with counsel, or with each other, but those nine men are being paid by the taxpayers to sit up there and ask questions, and counsel is well advised to be ready to answer their questions—*any* questions.

Tony Amsterdam led off in the case of *Earnest James Aikens v. the State of California*. A walking encyclopedia on capital punishment, he probably approached the lectern with well-justified confidence.

He began by telling the Court that the central issue was how

165

far the state and federal legislatures could go on the death penalty issue without review by the Court—without a definitive interpretation of the Eighth Amendment.*

"The very existence of a clause like the Cruel and Unusual Punishment clause belies the idea that legislatures are totally free in their selection of legislative methods . . .," Amsterdam stated. In his view, the critical point was that the Eighth Amendment provided for the "evolving standards of decency" recognized by the Court in *Trop v. Dulles*.

He quickly got to the question of uniformity of punishment as a constitutional requirement. Penalties must be uniformly applied against all, he said, not just against "a few outcast pariahs." Selectivity of application makes any statute "inherently suspect."

Mr. Justice Stewart said that he was bothered by the fact that the Constitution expressly recognized capital punishment. How could the Court now say that it was unconstitutional?

The Constitution *permits* the death penalty, Mr. Amsterdam replied; it doesn't *require* it and, again, "evolving standards of decency" show that the public conscience has changed. He referred to the "exceeding rarity" of the actual use of the death penalty. Even *before* the abolitionists started their moratorium, death sentences had dropped to about 100 per year.

Ronald M. George, deputy attorney general for the state of California, came up next. He had won the *McGautha* case for California the year before and his brilliance as an advocate matches Amsterdam's. (He is now a judge in Los Angeles County.)

First, he said, the Court should focus on the question of whether the federal Constitution could bar a state from executing people. Did the California legislature have a rational basis for concluding that it is proper to protect society from dangerous people by executing them for heinous crimes?

Mr. Justice Stewart asked if torture—"disembowelment, burning at the stake"—would not be deterrents.

*The following description of the oral argument in the *Furman* series of cases is taken from "Arguments Heard," a summary of the arguments appearing in the *Criminal Law Reporter*, January 26, 1972, vol. 10, p. 4146 ff. I have not set down all of the arguments, just the highlights. Unless quotation marks are used, I have paraphrased the colloquy between counsel and the Court.

Mr. George answered: "I do not think that capital punishment and torture necessarily have to stand or fall together . . ." Capital punishment, as used today, he said, would only be "cruel and unusual" if it were barbaric, or disproportionate to the offense.

He told the court that our "standards of decency" have not "evolved" to the point that Professor Amsterdam claimed. Forty-one states had capital punishment, public opinion polls certainly supported it, and juries continued to hand down death penalty verdicts.

He said that juries only imposed death for heinous crimes. They were "being discriminating, rather than discriminatory."

Amsterdam next got up to argue *Furman v. Georgia*. He said that Mr. George was right, 41 states still had the death penalty on the books, but they hadn't used it, thus indicating a trend that had led virtually every country in the world to abolish it. Juries only return about 100 death sentences a year, one out of every 12 or 13 cases in which death would be imposable.

He saw evidence of a nationwide repudiation of capital punishment and, again, signs of discrimination. When Mr. Justice Douglas asked him what kind of people Georgia executed, he replied: " . . . Georgia executes black people."

Mr. Justice Stewart got to the bottom line. Even if we assume that capital punishment is a deterrent, even if we are dealing with an incorrigible criminal and rational people could conclude that the death penalty is an effective sanction, you are still saying that it violates the Eighth Amendment?

Yes, Mr. Amsterdam said, the end doesn't justify the means.

Mrs. Dorothy Beasley, arguing for the state of Georgia, said that the Court, if it found capital punishment to be cruel and unusual by federal standards, would be rewriting the Fourteenth Amendment, which says that states can deprive people of life so long as due process of law is observed.

What standard would the state use, Mr. Justice Douglas asked.

"Fundamental fairness—fundamental to the concept of ordered liberty," she replied.

Jack Greenberg of the LDF argued on behalf of Lucious Jackson, sentenced to death for rape in Georgia. He declared flatly that the punishment for rape was disproportionate to the crime,

167

and therefore cruel and unusual. Citing statistics, he added that juries in Georgia discriminated against black defendants.

Mrs. Beasley countered. She disputed the claim of discrimination, but, she said, even if it existed, the problem was in the selection of juries themselves, who might or might not have been prejudiced. This was the area in which the problem should be attacked; not by abolishing the death penalty.

Mr. Greenberg, arguing in rebuttal, was asked by the chief justice: "Do you consider that a punishment is 'unusual' just because it is infrequent?"

That certainly is one meaning, Mr. Greenberg assured him.

Mr. Bruder of Dallas, arguing for Elmer Branch, sentenced to die for rape, agreed with Mr. Greenberg that executions for that crime were unusual in their infrequency and produced statistics of his own that the penalty was discriminatory.

Professor Charles Alan Wright, appearing for the state of Texas, zeroed in on the argument whether the death penalty itself was unconstitutional if it was only applied in rare cases. Either it is or it isn't, he asserted. If we can say that a presidential assassin or a bomber of a 747 can be executed, we cannot say that death is so inherently cruel as to be unconstitutional.

No advocate knows, when he walks out of the Supreme Court's hearing chamber, whether he has won or lost his case. The questions asked by the justices *may* give some indication which side they lean toward; but, quite often, they like to play the devil's advocate.

In the last colloquy of the *Furman* series of cases, for example, Mr. Justice Marshall asked defense counsel Bruder, during his rebuttal argument: "Then you would argue that the death penalty for treason is unconstitutional?"

Yes, said Mr. Bruder.

Mr. Justice Marshall: "What about treason that results in the cost of 10,000 soldiers?"

A good point, but we know from his later opinion in the *Furman* case that Justice Marshall thinks that the death penalty for *anything* is cruel and unusual punishment *per se*. The only time that you know that you have won (or lost) a case in the United States Supreme Court is when the Court tells you so by handing down a decision.

Michael Meltsner tells us that a mood of depression had set-tled down on the LDF attorneys just prior to the announcement of the *Furman* decision. Rumors were out that the abolitionists were going to lose by a 6–3 or 5–4 margin.[9]

But that's all they were: rumors. The security at the Supreme Court is amazing. We live in an age when the most private, high-level presidential conversations are the source of break-fast-table reading in the newspapers almost before they are ut-tered. The Congress of the United States couldn't keep its mouth shut if it had top-secret information that, revealed, would subject the United States to absolute domination by Liechtenstein.

But the Supreme Court is something else. In seven years of litigating before the Court, I have *never* known a decision to be leaked in advance.

At any rate, the LDF boys were morose and restive. They feared defeat and were already making contingency plans, as they had after *McGautha-Crampton*.

Then June 29, 1972 rolled around and they won. They really won! The rejoicing in the abolitionist camp has been described (see Chapter 1). Grinning murderers were shown on network television as they prepared to move off death row. Maybe they were smiling in relief that their lives had been spared; maybe they were laughing at the criminal-justice system in the United States and working out escape routes. Anyway, the abolition-ists had won. The only thing remaining was to read the Court's opinion and see how big they had won.

It all depended on how you looked at it. They had either won big or they had won, but . . . ? To be sure, they had saved 631 lives—and that's big. But the more thoughtful of the abolition-ists may have looked at the lineup on the Court. If, as many commentators stated when *Furman* was first announced, capi-tal punishment was constitutionally banned in this country for-ever, *those* numbers did not seem to bear it out.

Each justice had written a separate opinion, a rarity in Su-preme Court jurisprudence. After one had sifted through all the fine print, a read-out went something like this:

- Capital punishment is cruel and unusual and should be banned forever: two votes, Brennan and Marshall.

- Capital punishment *should* be cruel and unusual and banned forever but prior rulings of this Court say it isn't. Therefore I vote against it now only because it discriminates against minorities: one vote, Douglas.
- Capital punishment is not cruel and unusual *per se* but only as it is now applied because it is arbitrary: two votes, Stewart and White.
- Capital punishment is not cruel and unusual and the states are best left to their own devices in this area: four votes, Burger, Blackmun, Rehnquist, and Powell.

To summarize:

Capital punishment is gone forever	2
Capital punishment is not gone forever	4
Go back to the drawing board	3

This obviously oversimplifies. Each of the opinions was well thought out and, from the point of view of the writer, persuasively reasoned. A more detailed look is needed.

Mr. Justice Brennan came up with four principles by which he found the death penalty to be cruel and unusual punishment:

> In sum, the punishment of death is inconsistent with ... four principles. Death is an unusually severe and degrading punishment; there is a strong possibility that it is inflicted arbitrarily; its rejection by contemporary society is virtually total, and there is no reason to believe that it serves any penal purpose more effectively than the less severe punishment of imprisonment. The function of these principles is to enable a court to determine whether a punishment comports with human dignity. Death, quite simply, does not.[10]

If this sounds like a sociological treatise, that's because it is. The framers of the Constitution did not empower the Supreme Court to decide what did or did not "comport with human dignity"; they empowered it to interpret the Constitution and laws of the United States. Well, Justice Brennan didn't, but it would do very little good to tell him so. He's there, and we're here, and under the present constitutional setup he has the full power of the Court to wield, no matter how egregiously.

Mr. Justice Marshall basically agreed with Justice Brennan, but he didn't phrase it quite so cavalierly. He thought that the death penalty, permissible in the past, was impermissible now, finding that it was excessive, served no legitimate purpose, and, he claimed (completely incorrectly): "It is morally unacceptable to the people of the United States . . ."[11]

He made an exhaustive analysis of the deterrence argument and concluded:

> Despite the fact that the abolitionists have not proved nondeterrence beyond a reasonable doubt, they have succeeded in showing by clear and convincing evidence that capital punishment is not necessary as a deterrent to crime in our society. That is all that they must do.[12]

He cast the burden of proof of deterrence squarely on the proponents. He cited no precedent for that and, as a matter of fact, he was challenged by the chief justice on that particular point; but as matters turned out, the proponents were apparently able to carry the burden four years later in Gregg v. Georgia.

Mr. Justice Douglas, in a rare instance of judicial restraint, felt bound by McGautha and Crampton, so he could not find the penalty "cruel and unusual" per se. But:

> It would seem incontestable that the death penalty inflicted on one defendant is "unusual" if it discriminates against him by reason of his race, religion, wealth, social position, or class, or if it is imposed under a procedure that gives room for the play of such prejudices.[13]

Potter Stewart and Byron White, the "swing" justices, would not go so far as to say the penalty was unconstitutional. But, they said, it was, to use a few of their terms, so "wantonly," "freakishly," "capriciously," "infrequently," imposed that it had little or no retributive or deterrent value, and for that reason was cruel and unusual punishment.

The thoughtful abolitionist, however, reading between the lines of the two justices' opinions, might have found ominous the phrase of Justice White: "as it is presently administered . . ."[14] Here was a clear invitation to the states to come back with something that met the two justices' objections. How this was to be done wasn't spelled out clearly; nevertheless, there was a lot of leeway there. . . .

The four dissenters in *Furman*—Chief Justice Burger and Justices Blackmun, Powell, and Rehnquist—accused the majority variously of usurping the legislative power of the several states, misinterpreting the Constitution, misinterpreting the statistics on deterrence, misinterpreting the nature and force of public opinion, and quite generally going on a sort of constitutional rampage.

Although the chief justice and Justice Blackmun both asserted their personal opposition to capital punishment, it was clear beyond cavil from the tenor of their dissenting opinions that they were not about to impose their personal feelings on a nation of 200 million people (as had Justice Brennan) and that they felt strongly that the *Furman* majority was ill-advised, that the majority had decided wrongly and had done a super-number on the doctrine of separation of powers.

The thoughtful abolitionist reading *Furman*, then, could only conclude that there were four *very* hard votes against his position already on record. If anyone chose to accept the invitation of Justices Stewart and White to come up with some nonarbitrary and nondiscriminatory death penalty legislation, the tremendous abolitionist victory could go right down the tubes.

That was in the future, however. The LDF attorneys and their colleagues had every reason to be pleased and proud of themselves. They had parachuted into Normandy on D-Day. They fought against the odds and won. Brilliant, compassionate men, they had accomplished a legal coup that would go down in history.

But the little clouds on the horizon had coalesced. They were dark and foreboding now. Climatic conditions were perfect. Small heat-lightning flashes had turned into big ones. A thunderstorm of public opinion was about to break, and if the abolitionists cavorting in the wake of *Furman* didn't notice it, it was their own fault.

172

Notes

1. Michael Meltsner, *Cruel and Unusual*, New York: Random House (1973), p. 247.
2. *Ibid.*
3. *Ibid.*, p. 248.
4. *Ibid.*
5. *Ibid.*, p. 247.
6. *Ibid.*, pp. 249–251.
7. *Ibid.*, pp. 255–257.
8. *Ibid.*, pp. 253–254.
9. *Ibid.*, p. 286.
10. 408 U.S. 238, at page 305.
11. *Ibid.*, p. 260.
12. *Ibid.*, p. 253.
13. *Ibid.*, p. 242.
14. *Ibid.*, p. 312.

CHAPTER 12

Gregg v. Georgia:
Losing The War

The legislatures got busy almost as soon as *Furman* was
decided. Justice Brennan's assertion that contemporary society had almost totally rejected the death penalty was
mocked by the speed and force of the reaction to the decision.

Michael Meltsner, one of the principal architects of the LDF
strategy, described how some people responded:

> By the time the evening papers were out, a few congress-
> men had proposed an amendment to the Constitution in
> order to permit the death penalty. Several state legislative
> leaders said they would ask for laws sentencing convicted
> murderers to life imprisonment without possibility of pa-
> role. Georgia State Representative Sam Nunn, Jr., a candi-
> date for the United States Senate, announced that the deci-
> sion justified forcing federal judges to face the voters every
> six years. Not to be outdone, the *New York Daily News*
> urged state legislators to readopt the death penalty with all
> its "old-time" severity in order to see see "what the Su-
> preme Court does about that."[1]

174

Furman was decided in June of 1972; and it was apparent by then that the proponents of capital punishment in the state of California, outraged by the California Supreme Court's nullification of the death penalty in that state, had enough votes (over a million) to put the question to the test in a popular referendum aimed at restoring capital punishment. As we know, the citizens of California on November 7, 1972 voted in favor of the referendum by a two-to-one margin.*

In December 1972 the Florida legislature met in special session and adopted new death penalty legislation designed to comply with the *Furman* requirements. Pretty fast work, considering the tortoise-like pace at which state legislative bodies usually move.[2]

Ohio was next, in January 1973. The state's criminal code was revised to provide for capital punishment with a scheme similar to Florida's.[3]

By 1973 abolitionist Douglas Lyons, who runs an outfit called Citizens Against Legalized Murder, reported that bills to restore the death penalty would be introduced in three-fourths of the former capital punishment states *and* in Michigan, which had abolished some 127 years before.[4]

The good old "evolving standards of decency" theory was getting hit between the eyes; unless, of course, you took the position that the only credible judges of what was "decent" were the abolitionists themselves, a theory to which they heartily subscribe.

Except for the certainty that death incapacitates the person executed, thus preventing him from committing more murders, there are few other *certainties* in the entire area of the capital punishment debate. *Furman* created two: the fact that one or more states would restore capital punishment in an attempt to

*Commenting on the referendum, Meltsner stated that *Furman* would probably provoke a "considerable know-nothing vote . . ." (p. 307). There it is again. The old "we're-right-and-good-and-you're-just-a-bunch-of-know-nothings" syndrome. I can admire the brilliance of a man like Professor Meltsner, and his book *Cruel and Unusual* is one of the best things around from the abolitionists' point of view; but, why, oh why, can't they ever concede that people whose compassion is directed towards the *victims*, rather than their murderers, are something more than a bunch of cave dwellers?

comply with the Supreme Court's mandate (although it is difficult to imagine that even the most pessimistic abolitionist believed that so *many* would do it); and that these statutes would eventually be tested in the Supreme Court of the United States.

Now, whether the attitude in the state capitals was that "they're not going to push *us* around," or, more simply, that the death penalty was necessary to protect the innocent, *any* new capital punishment legislation would have to comply with the dictates of *Furman*. Specifically, with the dictates of Potter Stewart and Byron White.

Unless the states came up with something novel in the method of execution, like boiling in oil or drawing and quartering, which, of course, they weren't about to do, they could be reasonably certain that (assuming the makeup of the Court was still the same) they would have four hard votes to sustain their new capital punishment laws the next time the Supreme Court looked at them: the *Furman* dissenters—Chief Justice Burger and Justices Blackmun, Powell, and Rehnquist.

Justices William J. Brennan and Thurgood Marshall could pretty much be written off on the basis of what they had said in their opinions in the *Furman* case, as could Justice Douglas. That left Stewart and White, whose basic premise in *Furman* appeared to be that the *discretionary* aspect of sentencing to death, whether by judge or jury, automatically injected into the process enough randomness, capriciousness, and arbitrariness to render the whole thing unconstitutional.

Justice White reserved the question of the constitutionality of "statutes *requiring* the imposition of the death penalty for first degree murder, for more narrowly defined categories of murder, or for rape . . ."[5] Potter Stewart agreed. And the chief justice, in his dissenting opinion, provided some very helpful language when he stated his view that a state could define the worst classes of capital crime by

> providing standards for juries and judges to follow in determining the sentence in capital cases, or by more narrowly defining the crimes for which the penalty is to be imposed.[6]

So there was the problem: just what was the Court looking for? One thing was clear: *unfettered* discretion in the judge or jury was absolutely out. Now, the question was: do we do away with *all* discretion by narrowing the class of capital crimes and making the death penalty mandatory without reference to anything else, or do we narrow the class of crimes *and* the discretionary aspect by setting certain rigid standards that would greatly circumscribe the discretion of the judge and jury in handing out death sentences but would not make death an absolute (i.e., mandatory) in all capital cases?

Some states opted one way, some the other, and in 1976, when the Supreme Court came to grips with the problem in the Gregg series of cases, the statutes would stand or fall based on which option had been chosen.

Georgia, Florida, and Texas went the "standards" route and, as matters turned out, took the right path. Louisiana and North Carolina opted for mandatory sentences and lost out when a 5–4 majority of the Court found this unconstitutional.

Here are a few examples of the statutory schemes. Georgia was a "standards" state. In describing the Georgia statute, I shall paraphrase from the majority opinion of Justice Stewart in *Gregg v. Georgia*, the case in which that state's statutory system of capital sentencing was upheld.[7]

Georgia retains the death penalty for six categories of crime: murder, kidnapping for ransom or where the victim was harmed, armed robbery, rape, treason, and aircraft hijacking. * Murder is basically defined as causing the death of another unlawfully and with malice aforethought, express or implied.

The capital defendant is tried by a judge or by a jury in the regular manner. Naturally, if he is found innocent (or guilty of a less-than-capital crime), the matter is closed insofar as the death penalty is concerned. If the defendant is found guilty of the capital offense, or pleads guilty to it, he is then given a second hearing to determine what the penalty should be. This system is what is known as a "bifurcated system"; the first trial is called the "guilt stage," the presentence hearing is called the "penalty stage."

*I will confine the analysis to the crime of murder, as I have done throughout this book. The Supreme Court in the Gregg series of cases only upheld convictions for murder under the new state capital punishment statutes. The Court subsequently held in *Coker v. Georgia*, 97 S.Ct.2861 (1977) that the death penalty for rape was cruel and unusual.

The second, or presentence, hearing is held before whoever made the finding of guilty, judge or jury. The judge or jury hears additional evidence in aggravation or mitigation of punishment, including any record of prior convictions or absence thereof. The state can only introduce evidence of aggravation of the offense that it has made known to the defendant prior to his trial. The state and the defense may argue before the judge or jury regarding the punishment to be imposed.

This is what is meant by standards. The judge or jury in the sentencing process has *some* discretion whether to impose the death sentence or not, but this discretion is carefully circumscribed by the standards set out in the statutory sentencing scheme.

The judge or jury must find, beyond a reasonable doubt, one or more of ten circumstances that aggravate the crime sufficiently to justify the death penalty. The circumstances are:

1. The defendant had a prior record of conviction for a capital crime.
2. Murder in the commission of a felony.
3. The offender by his act of murder knowingly created a great risk of death to more than one person in a public place by a hazardous weapon or device.
4. The murder was committed for something of monetary value or for hire.
5. Murder of present or former judges or district attorneys because of the exercise of their official duties.
6. Causing or directing another to commit murder.
7. The offense was outrageously or wantonly vile, horrible, or inhuman in that it involved torture, depravity of mind, or an aggravated battery to the victim.
8. Murdering a peace officer, corrections officer, or fireman while in the performance of his official duties.
9. Murder by one who is in or has escaped from a peace officer or place of lawful confinement or custody.
10. The murder was committed to avoid, interfere with, or prevent a lawful arrest or lawful confinement.

These are, in actuality, standards within standards: the first standard is that guilt of the crime must be proven beyond a reasonable doubt; *then*, in order to impose death, the second set of standards—the ten circumstances in aggravation just noted

—must be applied and one or more found beyond a reasonable doubt. And of course, evidence in mitigation must also be heard.

If the sentence is death, the defendant has a special, direct, and expedited appeal to the Georgia Supreme Court, which, in addition to determining the more traditional questions of whether error occurred during the trial and whether the evidence supported a guilty verdict, must determine:

1. Whether the death sentence was imposed "under the influence of passion, prejudice or any other arbitrary factor";
2. Whether the evidence supports a finding of one or more of the ten "aggravating circumstances"; and
3. Whether the sentence is excessive or disproportionate to other sentences in similar cases considering the crime and the defendant.

Additionally, the Georgia Supreme Court, if it affirms the death sentence, must refer to similar cases that it has taken into consideration.

Finally, just to go that one step farther to ensure against arbitrary and discriminatory sentencing, the trial judge must submit to the Georgia Supreme Court a six-page report on the crime, the defendant, and the trial. The report gives detailed responses to questions concerning the quality of the defendant's representation, whether race played a role in the trial, and whether the trial court had satisfied itself about the appropriateness of the sentence.

The only better way to guarantee to a defendant that his death sentence was neither unfair, arbitrary, capricious, nor discriminatory would be to sentence by computer, and our criminal justice system hasn't gotten around to *that* yet.

The sentencing schemes in Texas and Florida, while not so elaborate as those of Georgia, provide both the narrowing of classes of capital crimes and the setting of standards (including aggravation and mitigation) that sufficiently circumscribe the element of discretion to pass Supreme Court muster as being in compliance with the dictates of *Furman*.

Louisiana and North Carolina elected to go the mandatory route. They narrowed their classes of capital crimes somewhat and then simply said that if the defendant was convicted of one

179

or more of these crimes, he must be sentenced to death, period. Of course, the capital defendant still had all of the traditional avenues of appeal available to him: did the evidence support the finding of his guilt? Was all the evidence used against him legally admissible (i.e., not a product of an "illegal" search and seizure or an involuntary confession)? Did he get a fair trial?

But the latter two states failed to come up with the innovations that Georgia, Florida, and Texas had. They did away with *all* discretion rather than provide standards to circumscribe *some* discretion; and that is where they made their mistake.

Not one particle of blame should attach to the legal draftsmen in Raleigh and Baton Rouge. They are guilty of nothing more than reading the *Furman* opinion too literally. Many attorneys and other practitioners in the criminal-justice system who had an interest in the capital punishment issue (this writer included) tended to believe that mandatory death sentences were the only answer to the *Furman* case.

Justices Stewart and White had made such a to-do over the discretionary aspects of capital sentencing that, for many of us, the obvious corollary was to remove discretion entirely and that means make it mandatory. I'm awfully glad that the people in Atlanta, Tallahassee, and Austin were able to read between the lines and to divine what Potter Stewart was really talking about (Justice White, ironically, dissented in the Louisiana and North Carolina cases and would have held the mandatory death sentences to be constitutional); but no one should cast any stones at Louisiana and North Carolina for not being clairvoyant.

We have Michael Meltsner's excellent book *Cruel and Unusual* to tell us how the abolitionists felt up to and after *Furman v. Georgia*, and there is no one who can speak with greater authority than a person like Mr. Meltsner, who participated in the case.

We have no such information about how the LDF and others felt when, in January of 1976, the Court agreed to hear the cases of *Gregg v. Georgia*, *Jurek v. Texas*, *Proffitt v. Florida*, *Woodson v. North Carolina*, and *Roberts v. Louisiana*.* The court

*See Chapter 1, notes 7 and 8 for case citations.

had heard arguments about the death penalty the previous year in a case called *Fowler v. North Carolina,* but it then apparently decided that it hadn't heard enough and ordered the *Gregg* series of cases consolidated for hearing.

We can be reasonably certain of one thing: the factual situations, from the abolitionist point of view, were not nearly as helpful in the *Gregg* series as they had been in *Furman.* In the *Furman* series, as we know, two defendants had been sentenced to die for the crime of rape and one for a murder that was accidental (though made capital because it occurred in the course of a house burglary). Only one of the defendants, Earnest Aikens, had been convicted of truly horrifying crimes: two disgusting rape-murders, one of a pregnant woman.

As I noted in the previous chapter, the Supreme Court isn't supposed to, and probably doesn't (to the extent humanly possible) take into consideration the depravity of the individual criminals whose cases are before it. But the lineup in the *Gregg* series certainly didn't *help* matters.

- Troy Leon Gregg (white), sentenced to death in Georgia for murdering two men, execution style, who had given him and a companion a lift. The motive was robbery; one of the good samaritans who picked up Gregg and his buddy had ill advisedly flashed a roll of money in front of him.
- Jerry Lane Jurek (white) received the death penalty in Texas for abducting a 10-year-old girl, choking her when she refused his sexual advances, and throwing her unconscious body into a river where it was recovered, drowned, two days later.
- Charles William Proffitt (white) was convicted and sentenced to die for murder in Florida after he plunged a butcher knife into the chest of Joel Medgebow during the course of a burglary.
- James Tyrone Woodson (black) received the death penalty in North Carolina for his part in an armed robbery of a convenience store, in the course of which a cashier was killed and a customer seriously wounded.
- Stanislaus Roberts (black), condemned after his conviction for the robbery-murder of a filling station owner in Lake Charles, Louisiana. Roberts shot his victim four times in the head.

181

Six innocent victims dead; five killers (whom, of course, the abolitionists consider "victims") condemned under post-*Furman* death penalty statutes. At stake in *Gregg* were the laws of those states that had enacted new capital punishment statutes after *Furman* arguably because escalating murder rates had turned the clouds of public sentiment for the death penalty into a raging thunderstorm. Death rows were again filling up after the *Furman* exodus, and it was high time that the Court took a look.

Briefs were filed and the same arguments used in the *Furman* series of cases were trotted out, but there were some new wrinkles. First, the abolitionists had to contend that even when jury discretion was circumscribed by set standards, even when the sentence was made mandatory, the death penalty was *still* arbitrary, capricious, and discriminatory.

In addition, the abolitionists would, for the first time, have no corner on the market for statistics in the argument over deterrence. The science of econometrics had entered the picture. People like Isaac Ehrlich, Gordon Tullock, and James Yunker were saying that *their* numbers indicated that each execution would save "x" number of lives. Nor did it matter that Professor Ehrlich was, personally, opposed to capital punishment on moral grounds. His findings on deterrence were there for all the world, and the Supreme Court, to see.

Then there were the public opinion polls, the California referendum, and the 35 new state capital punishment laws to deal with. The abolitionists could ignore them, or they could, if confronted with them, say that that sort of evidence "doesn't mean much." But it surely doesn't help the old "evolving standards of decency" argument, does it?

The *amicus curiae* briefs came trooping in; but this time some heavy artillery had been brought up in support of the proponents. The Court had asked Robert Bork, the solicitor general of the United States, to brief and argue the issue as *amicus curiae* for the government, and everyone knew where Bork, a brilliant conservative, stood.

Additionally, the Court, in a relatively rare move, granted leave for William E. James, assistant attorney general of the state of California, to argue as *amicus curiae* in support of the respondent states. Of course, the defendants' time would be increased by the same number of minutes that had been allotted to the *amici;* but people familiar with Supreme Court jurisprudence know that you have to get up *very* early in the morning to catch up with Bob Bork and Bill James.

Again the attorneys lined up for oral argument. More of them this time:

For the Petitioners

Jurek:	Anthony Amsterdam
Roberts:	Anthony Amsterdam
Woodson:	Anthony Amsterdam
Gregg:	G. Hughel Harrison, Lawrenceville, Georgia
Proffitt:	Clinton A. Curtis, Barstow, Florida

For the Respondents

State of Texas: Hon. John L. Hill, Attorney General

State of Louisiana: James Babin, Assistant District Attorney, Fourteenth Judicial District

State of North Carolina: Sidney S. Eagles, Jr., Assistant Attorney General

State of Georgia: G. Thomas Davis, Senior Assistant Attorney General

State of Florida: Hon. Robert L. Shevin, Attorney General

United States of America: Hon. Robert Bork, Solicitor General, as *amicus curiae*

State of California: William E. James, Assistant Attorney General, as *amicus curiae*

There was one new face on the Court. Mr. Justice Douglas had retired in 1975, and President Ford had appointed Judge John Paul Stevens of the U.S. Court of Appeals for the Seventh Circuit in Chicago to fill the vacancy. This was a blow to the abolitionist side. They could have been 95 percent certain of getting Justice Douglas' vote; now here was an unknown quantity.

Also on the minus side, from the abolitionist point of view: Justice Stevens was a moderate-conservative in his judicial philosophy, which meant they would have to convince him pretty thoroughly before he would vote to overturn, for a *second* time, the statutes of 35 states. On the plus side, the new Justice had a reputation for unusual brilliance and complete independence of mind. He *could* be convinced if the arguments were right; but it's never pleasant to lose a shoo-in vote for one that can't be predicted.

Two days, March 30 and 31, 1976, were set for oral argument. The justices would have blinked and stared about them in wonder if anyone but Tony Amsterdam had led off. He did.

He outlined for the Court the state of the death penalty since *Furman*: 35 states and the United States (for air piracy) had enacted new capital punishment laws.* He categorized the statutes: the Florida and Georgia types provide for a two-step proceeding, one for guilt and one for punishment with consideration of aggravating and mitigating circumstances; Texas requires the finding of a specific fact, occurence, or condition before death can be imposed; Louisiana requires a similar finding but it is built into the definition of the crime itself; and North Carolina simply makes a death sentence mandatory upon conviction of certain capital crimes.

Amsterdam then told the Court that the new statutes were still arbitrary and capricious and, anyway, the death penalty was *per se* cruel and unusual punishment.

He contended that because the new statutes were so narrowly drawn, there was an "elaborate winnowing process" with many outlets for avoiding the death penalty. Hence we are back where we were before *Furman:* the death sentence is imposed randomly and arbitrarily.

The chief justice asked if no statute could ever meet the requirements of *Furman*. Amsterdam answered that that was what he was arguing. He said, moreover, that the arbitrariness condemned in *Furman* was built into the new statutes. He singled out the Texas statute for particular criticism.

What about *McGautha*, asked Mr. Justice Stewart, where the Court said that juries could have discretion in sentencing? That was a due-process case, Amsterdam said; what we're talking

*The following description of the highlights of the oral argument in the *Gregg* series of cases is taken from "Arguments Heard," a summary of the arguments appearing in the *Criminal Law Reporter*, volume 19, p. 4005 ff., April 7, 1976. Statements by counsel and the Court are paraphrased unless quotation marks are used.

184

about now is an across-the-board Eighth Amendment application to all capital cases.

Mr. Justice Stevens asked if the degree of discretion depended on the number of crimes defined as capital and the breadth of the definition.

The narrower the definition, the more arbitrary will be the distinctions made by the jury, Professor Amsterdam replied.

Attorney General John L. Hill of Texas said that the statute in that state did not result in the selectivity condemned in *Furman*, and, he added, no statute could or should remove *all* discretion. He defended the Texas scheme that requires a specific finding that the defendant intended the killing, that he would likely commit more crimes of violence in the future, and that he responded unreasonably to provocation, before death could be imposed. He cited the horrible nature of Jurek's crime and defended the death sentence imposed for it.

James Babin argued for Louisiana, challenging Amsterdam's contention that juries are not dependable. They take an oath and they perform their duties, he said. To attack the entire jury system is unreasonable.

William E. James, arguing for California as *amicus curiae*, made three points: 1) he asked the Court to confirm the constitutionality of capital punishment, 2) he suggested that the Court furnish guidelines for the states as to sentencing procedures, and 3) he told about the two-to-one referendum victory for capital punishment produced by the California voters.

Solicitor General Robert Bork argued as *amicus curiae* on behalf of the United States. His major thesis was that the legislative reaction to *Furman*—reinstatement of the death penalty—clearly indicated that capital punishment is not out of step with current morality, and that is where the Court should look, "not to the writings of the more enlightened professors."

As to the charge that the penalty was "unusual": "I do not see how capital punishment can be unconstitutional just because it is used carefully."

Bork then attacked Professor Amsterdam's theories about discretion. He told the Court that the abolitionist argument seemed to be that *any* system that allows discretion is unconstitutional. "The more counsel explains this argument, the less I understand it," he said.

185

He told the Court that the death penalty deters, and then he got some help from Mr. Justice Powell:

> While I recognize that deterrence may not be the controlling factor here, I invite your attention to the 1973 report of the FBI showing that murder has increased 42 percent between 1968 and 1973. It is fairly obvious that we need some way to deter this slaughter of Americans. I say "slaughter" because that word was used in describing the American death toll during our involvement in Vietnam. Comparing the records of Vietnam and the FBI's figures, it appears that, on an annual basis, more Americans are murdered in this country than were killed in Vietnam. Do you care to comment?

Bork, no fool, agreed. He replied that common sense tells us that death is a deterrent: as we increase the cost and risk of certain conduct, the incidence of that conduct will decrease. The Court, he said pointedly, would take upon itself an awesome responsibility if it were to condemn thousands of potential murder victims in order to save a few hundred guilty people.

Professor Amsterdam returned, in *Woodson v. North Carolina,* to his bottom-line argument: "Capital punishment is atavistic butchery which has run its course."

Could Mr. Amsterdam conceive of no crime that would deserve the death penalty? asked Mr. Justice Powell. The answer was no.

"Suppose a terrorist destroys New York City with a hydrogen bomb?"

Still no, Amsterdam replied, adding irrelevantly that such crimes can be prevented through police methods rather than fear of punishment.

Sidney Eagles spoke for North Carolina. We must have the ultimate deterrent, he argued, to prevent crimes. "Domestic tranquility, one of the great objectives of government," does not mean much to the victim of a heinous crime.

In rebuttal Amsterdam told the chief justice that public opinion polls should not be taken into consideration when the Court is deciding capital punishment cases. The chief justice replied that he thought that the Court was supposed to view the death penalty in light of the public's moral views.

No, and not in light of the fact that 35 states have adopted new capital punishment laws, either, was the reply.

G. Hughel Harrison, arguing for the defendant in *Gregg v. Georgia*, told the Court that there was still too much discretion embodied in that state's statute and that it simply did not satisfy the *Furman* standard.

G. Thomas Davis, for the Georgia attorney general's office, countered: Look at the record. A review of Georgia cases demonstrates that the statute is working rationally and the distinctions made between defendants, which under Georgia law must be reviewed by the Georgia Supreme Court, are, indeed, supportable.

Clinton Curtis, arguing on behalf of Proffitt, alleged that the Florida statute was unconstitutional because the standards governing appellate review of a death sentence were meaningless.

Robert L. Shevin, attorney general of the state of Florida, may have had personal as well as professional feelings when he began his argument: his father had been murdered a number of years ago in the course of a robbery. He defended the Florida system in all of its particulars; he thought it was fair to the accused in all respects. So much so, he told the Court, that he was not asking that *Furman* be reversed; we are satisfied with our current procedure.

Then the waiting period; and then the decision, on July 2, 1976, upholding the constitutionality of capital punishment generally and the statutes of Florida, Georgia, and Texas in particular. The abolitionists who had flown so high when *Furman* was decided almost exactly four years before were crestfallen. They seemed to find an arcane connection between the date of the decision and the fact that the nation's Bicentennial was two days away, and commented sarcastically that it was some birthday present for the country. For all but the abolitionists, it was pretty clear that "standards of decency" in the United States had not evolved much in 200 years.

In the *Gregg* series of decisions, seven justices held that capital punishment itself did not violate the Eighth Amendment. They were Justice Stewart, who wrote the opinions; the Chief Justice Burger; and Justices White, Blackmun, Powell, Rehnquist, and Stevens. Justices Brennan and Marshall dissented. They still felt that the death penalty was unconstitutionally cruel and unusual.

The head count was the same with regard to the particular

187

statutes of Georgia, Florida, and Texas that allowed some discretion in sentencing judges and juries but that circumscribed this discretion with carefully defined standards so that the imposition of the penalty would not be arbitrary or discriminatory.

The Court split 5–4 on the mandatory death penalty statutes of Louisiana and North Carolina. Three justices—Stewart, Stevens, and Powell—felt that a mandatory death penalty was cruel and unusual because it provided no objective standards for the imposition of the penalty. Justices Brennan and Marshall naturally joined these three.

The chief justice, joined by Justices White, Blackmun, and Rehnquist, found no such fault with the North Carolina and Louisiana statutes. But they were outvoted.

The decision in *Gregg* is one of enormous significance. The Court has held with finality that the Eighth Amendment does not bar the death penalty. The 50 states are now free to enact capital punishment laws if they wish to. Of course, the laws that they enact must be constitutional, but, by upholding the Georgia/Florida/Texas trilogy of statutes, the Court has given a blueprint to all other states. It has told them what *is* constitutional. The abolitionists will continue their battle on a case-by-case basis, but with the constitutional door now closed to them, and public opinion now inflamed by our skyrocketing homicide rates, it is unlikely that they will be able to impose another moratorium on executions in the United States.

As we did with the *Furman* case, we must look at just what the Court said in the *Gregg* series. Justice Potter Stewart wrote all of the majority opinions, thus irrevocably casting himself in the role as the Court's preeminent jurist in this area.

The basic question whether capital punishment is cruel and unusual under the Eighth Amendment was answered by Justice Stewart in *Gregg v. Georgia*. No.

Justice Stewart began his analysis by noting that, historically, the framers of the Constitution recognized capital punishment and that the Court itself had never held it invalid *per se*. Only "excessive" punishment, that which unnecessarily inflicts suffering or is disproportionate to the offense. And, although a legislature may not impose such "excessive" punishment, it is not required to impose the *least* severe penalty.

He then examined the "evolving standards of decency" arguments and found them wanting.

> Four years ago, the petitioners in *Furman* and its companion cases predicated their argument primarily upon the asserted proposition that standards of decency had evolved to the point where capital punishment no longer could be tolerated.[8]

Right. And the argument carried some weight then. But the abolitionists chose to blind themselves to the mounting rates of homicide and the resultant hardening of public opinion. They could, if they wished, ignore this, but the equation was forming:

HOMICIDE RATES + PUBLIC REACTION = LEGISLATIVE SUPPORT FOR THE DEATH PENALTY

And it was this legislative support, embodied in 35 state laws, that convinced Justice Stewart:

> The petitioners in the capital cases before the Court today renew the "standards of decency" argument, but developments during the four years since *Furman* have undercut substantially the assumptions upon which the argument rested. Despite the continuing debate, dating back to the 19th century, over the morality and utility of capital punishment, it is now evident that a large percentage of American society continues to regard it as an appropriate and necessary criminal sanction.
>
> The most marked indication of society's endorsement of the death penalty for murder is the legislative response to *Furman*. The legislatures of 35 states have enacted new statutes that provide for the death penalty for at least some crimes that result in the death of another person.[9]

He also referred to the California referendum, public opinion polls, and the fact that by the end of March 1976, four hundred sixty persons had filled the places of their happier predecessors, who had been spared by *Furman*, on death row.

One wonders. Were the abolitionists so sure of their rightness that they simply blinded themselves to the fact that public opinion was wiping out one of their strongest arguments? Or didn't they care?

Justice Stewart then dealt with the two major justifications

189

for capital punishment: retribution and deterrence. (Discussed above in Chapters 8 and 5, respectively.) He found merit in both.

He specifically limited his reasoning to murder cases (as does this book); but in such cases, he said for the majority of the Court:

> We hold that the death penalty is not a form of punishment that may never be imposed, regardless of the circumstances of the offense, regardless of the character of the offender, and regardless of the procedure followed in reaching the decision to impose it.[10]

Justice Stewart then turned his attention to the Georgia statute in question. Did it meet the demands of the *Furman* decision? It did. It provided for specific findings with regard to the circumstances of the crime and the character of the defendant. Review by the Georgia Supreme Court was automatic, expedited, and exhaustive.

The conclusion:

> For the reasons expressed in this opinion, we hold that the statutory system under which Gregg was sentenced to death does not violate the Constitution.[11]

Similarly, with some factual variations, the capital punishment laws of Florida and Texas were upheld. The basic rule was this: if adequate standards are set up to ensure that the decision to impose capital punishment is rational, if it will be applied as uniformly as it can be in a system run by human beings, if no extraneous factors such as race—*particularly* race— go into the decision-making process, and if review at the highest state-court level is provided as a sort of fail-safe system, then the statutes are constitutional.

The "mandatory" states ran afoul of this rubric precisely because they did *not* provide the standards. With regard to North Carolina, Justice Stewart stated that its

> mandatory death penalty statute provides no standards to guide the jury in its inevitable exercise of the power to determine which first-degree murderers shall live and which shall die.[12]

Essentially the same thing was wrong with Louisiana's statute,* although, as we have noted, four justices couldn't see much difference between the two statutes struck down and the three that were upheld.

In all five cases, Justices Brennan and Marshall stuck to their view that capital punishment was cruel and unusual *per se*, just as they had held in *Furman v. Georgia*. The only difference was that in *Gregg*, they were writing for a two-justice minority.

The important thing was that the constitutional question had been decided, and by a solid 7–2 majority.

So, capital punishment is with us again, at least on paper. The moratorium is over, at least in the constitutional sense. We have seen how a minority of people—the abolitionists, self-appointed keepers of the nation's conscience—could thwart the will of the majority for years.

But we have also seen how the United States Supreme Court, not the *self*-appointed, but the *constitutionally* appointed keeper of the nation's legal conscience, responded. Capital punishment was not cruel and unusual when the Constitution was written, it told the abolitionists, and if you want us to embrace those nebulous "evolving standards of decency," you had better show us some numbers.

The abolitionists didn't *have* any numbers; in fact, the numbers all went the other way: the polls, the referenda, and the 36 reinstatements (35 state and one federal) of the death penalty could be ignored by the abolitionists only because they knew that *they*, and they alone, were right. But the Court was not about to ignore the signs of the times.

There were some other numbers, too. The unbelievable jump in homicide rates since the moratorium: 12,000 plus when the moratorium began to 20,000 plus in 1975. *Those figures* don't mean anything, the abolitionists said. They do to *me*, said Justice Powell when he asked how else we were going to "deter this slaughter."

I said earlier that the bottom line was victims' rights vs. the

*The Court in 1977 looked at the constitutionality of narrowly drawn statutes that mandate death for the murder of a policeman. In a 5–4 decision if reaffirmed its earlier position that mandatory statutes are unconstitutional. *Harry Roberts v. Louisiana*, 97 S.Ct. 1993 (1977).

191

rights of convicted murderers. The Court showed in *Gregg* whose side *it* was on, and in the long run that is all that really matters.

Now it's up to the states. They can, constitutionally, begin to execute murderers. Utah has already done so. If others do, and *if* (I emphasize the if) death is perceived as an actual threat, so that capital punishment causes the homicide rates to go down, then the potential victims who have been spared by that threat will have been well served.

Of course, it may not happen that way.

But it's worth a try.

Notes

1. Michael Meltsner, *Cruel and Unusual*; New York: Random House (1973), p. 291.
2. *Ibid.*, p. 307.
3. *Ibid.*, pp. 307–308.
4. *Ibid.*, p. 308.
5. 408 U.S. 238 at 311.
6. 408 U.S. 238 at 401.
7. 428 U.S. 153, 96 S. Ct. 2909 at page 2920 (1976).
8. 428 U.S. 153, 96 S. Ct. 2909 at 2928 (1976).
9. *Ibid.*
10. *Ibid.* at 2932.
11. *Ibid.* at 2941.
12. *Ibid.* at 2991.

APPENDIX A

Capital Punisment Deters Crime *

There is an inherent logic to the belief that the death penalty deters at least some people from committing crimes. "Belief in the deterrent efficacy of penal sanctions is as old as the criminal law itself." Zimring & Hawkins, *Deterrence* 1 (1973). Just as some penalty deters a prospective offender by making the prospect of crime less attractive, so does a more severe penalty make crime still less attractive, and so less likely to occur.[1] Because death is perceived by most potential law breakers as the maximum feasible penalty, it is probably the most effective deterrent force. "*Prima facie* the penalty of death is likely to have a stronger effect as a deterrent to normal human beings than any other form a punishment. . . ." Royal Commission on Capital Punishment, *1949-1953 Report*, par. 61 (1953). It is not unreasonable or insupportable for a legislature to credit an argument with such strong plausibility.

*Appendices A and B are taken from the brief *amicus curiae* filed by the United States in support of the state of Georgia in *Gregg v. Georgia*.

193

The primary arguments against the deterrent force of capital punishment are that criminals (by definition) are not "normal" people, and so do not respond in "normal" ways, and that many murders or other capital crimes are crimes of passion and hence not deterrable. Neither argument supports a conclusion that capital punishment does not have a deterrent effect. The only surface evidence that criminals are not "normal" is their failure to conform to some social "norms"; that evidence alone is not proof (or even support) for the proposition that "criminals" do not respond to incentives, to the prospect of pain or pleasure.[2]

We can conclude, perhaps, that those who do not obey the laws have little respect for the law *per se*, and in that sense lack a "normal" trait. But we cannot conclude that all criminals are completely insensitive to deterrence merely because they commit crimes; we can validly conclude only that they have evaluated the prospects of success (and the "cost" to them of apprehension) differently from those who have the propensity to offend but do not. See Packer, *The Limits of the Criminal Sanction* 40–45 (1968). Indeed, the efforts of most criminals to avoid detection, and to escape after being caught, show very clearly that they are sensitive to a calculus of pains and pleasures.

Similarly, although there are many crimes committed in such intense passion that the offender may altogether neglect to consider the prospect of punishment in the future, the existence of such people and such crimes of passion does not indicate that there are no deterrable crimes. Some murders are committed for money, some after lengthy contemplation. Treason, espionage, sabotage, aircraft piracy, and deliberate wrecking of trains (all of them federal capital offenses) are prime examples of entire categories of offense committed after calculation and in pursuit of ulterior goals. The people who commit such crimes are rational (albeit misguided or evil) individuals, and there is no reason to believe they will not attend their own self-interest and consider the potential severity of the penalty that might be meted out in response. These crimes (at least) are sufficiently narrow and clearly defined, and sufficiently open to dissuasion by deterrence, that capital punishment is permissible for them regardless of its deterrent value as applied to other crimes.[3] The death penalty could realistically be made a fully predictable re-

194

sponse to these crimes, and those contemplating such criminal activity could be required to take into account a very great probability of execution if caught.

Moreover, although an individual may use a weapon in a fit of passion, the decision to carry a weapon at all is made with a cool head and (often) considerable forethought. The prospect that he will find himself unable or unwilling to control the use of that weapon may cause many people not to possess or carry it, and consequently decrease the number of "passionate" killings. Legislators may also legitimately conclude that many crimes committed in passion are deterrable even if some are not, and that the death penalty is appropriately applied to the entire category to save as many innocent lives as possible. The choice of crimes for which capital punishment is to be authorized is, unless indisputably aberrant and grossly disproportionate, a legislative choice.

Legislators are not alone in believing that the death penalty is a more effective deterrent than is life imprisonment. A recent study has tentatively concluded that when capital punishment was *actually used* a significant number of lives were saved: over the period studied, and after controlling for the effects of other variables, using the death penalty instead of imprisonment may have deterred approximately eight murders for each execution actually carried out. See Ehrlich, "The Deterrent Effect of Capital Punishment," 65 *American Economic Review* 397 (1975).[4] Two statisticians, although critical of some of Professor Ehrlich's technical methods, have duplicated his results; using data other than those used by Ehrlich, these investigators produced "results . . . similar to Ehrlich's." Bowers and Pierce, "The Illusion of Deterrence in Isaac Ehrlich's Research on Capital Punishment," 85 *Yale Law Journal* 187, 196 (1975) (footnote omitted). Moreover, another recent study, using methodology significantly different from Ehrlich's, has concluded that Ehrlich actually underestimated the deterrent force of capital punishment by a factor of five "and that the evidence is better consistent with the view that one execution will deter at least 50 homicides." Yunker, "The Deterrent Effect of Capital Punishment: Comment" (unpublished manuscript). See also Schuessler, "The Deterrent Influence of the Death Penalty," 284 *Annals* 54, 60 (1952) ("The correlation between these two indices [the number of executions per 1,000 homicides and the homicide rate in 41 death penalty states] was -.26, indicating a slight tendency for the homicide rate to diminish as the probability of execution increases.") These studies provide important empirical support for the *a priori* logical belief that the use of the death penalty decreases the number of murders.

Other studies of the deterrent value of the death penalty (see, e.g., Sellin, *The Death Penalty* (1959)) have not concluded that there is proof that capital punishment deters crimes. But neither have they supplied proof that it fails to deter. Zimring & Hawkins, *supra*, at 254–255, 257–258. All of the earlier studies that have found no measurable deterrent effect from the death penalty have shared certain investigatory flaws. For example, these studies have relied not upon the actual use of the death penalty, but upon its statutory authorization, as the independent variable against which the murder rate was compared.[5] The effects of mere statutory authorization of capital punishment tell us nothing about the effects of its use, as Sellin himself admitted. Sellin, *supra*, at 20. All of the studies have evaluated the effect of the death penalty on the overall murder rate, rather than on the rate of capital murders, and so the studies cannot exclude the possibility that the death penalty deters the commission of those murders to which it applies.[6] None of the studies has attempted to isolate the effect of the death penalty on special and highly deterrable capital crimes, such as murder for hire. And, perhaps most importantly, all of the earlier studies failed to hold constant factors other than the death penalty that might influence the rate of murders. Only if the death penalty is the sole determinant of the murder rate, or if other determinants are identical in states having different execution rates, would it be proper to infer from these studies that the death penalty has no deterrent effect.[7]

But states—even the contiguous states studied by Sellin— have important differences. Indeed, these very differences may explain why one state chooses to use the death penalty and another does not, and still other differences might have an independent effect directly on the rate of violent crime. Or suppose that a state that had abolished capital punishment also had a high arrest and conviction rate for murder, so that although a murderer would be punished less severely, his expectation of net punishment would be greater in this state than in a state with capital punishment but a low arrest and conviction rate. Unless factors such as this are held constant—as the most recent studies have done—no valid conclusions may be drawn. As one opponent of capital punishment has remarked about the previous studies:

> The inescapable flaw is, of course, that social conditions in any state are not constant through time, and that social conditions are not the same in any two states. If an effect [from the presence or absence of capital punishment] were observed (and the observed effects, one way or another, are not large) then one could not at all tell whether any of this effect is attributable to the presence or absence of capital punishment. A "scientific"—that is to say, a soundly based—conclusion is simply impossible. . . . [Black, *Capital Punishment: The Inevitability of Caprice and Mistake* 25–26 (1974).]

Professor Passell, upon whom petitioners rely (*Jurek* Pet. Br. App. 2, Sub-app. E), agrees. He has written: "It cannot be proven that executions do not serve as a deterrent to murder. Proof is simply beyond the capacities of empirical social science." Passell, "The Deterrent Effect of the Death Penalty: A Statistical Test," 28 *Stanford Law Review* 61, 79 (1975). And, he writes (*ibid.* at 62–63), "even were one to accept without qualification the validity of the [pre-Ehrlich] research designs and the accuracy of the data employed, their evidence against deterrence could not be considered conclusive."

The older studies suggesting that capital punishment has no observable deterrent effect are deficient in yet another respect. Their results may have been produced by an entirely practical problem: the real deterrent value of capital punishment may be sufficiently small in relation to the number of murders committed each year that it is difficult to detect, given the deficiencies in data gathering (many crimes are not reported, and changes in the reporting rate are impossible to detect; in some cases it is difficult to determine whether a particular death is a "murder") and the very bulk of the raw data. In recent years there have been more than 15,000 murders per year,[8] so that even if one execution deterred 10 murders, the effect on the murder rate might become lost in the statistical "noise."

197

We submit that the states are entitled to make use of the death penalty even if the effects are "small" in comparison to the gross murder rate. We do not imply by this argument that the deterrent value of capital punishment is "small" in human terms; every murder is supremely important to the victim and to his or her family and acquaintances. Indeed, it is supremely important to society, its morale, its sense of community, its sense of the security not only of lives but of values. Suppose that a state finds it necessary to impose the death penalty only a few (two, three or four) times yearly on the worst offenders. In all probability the resultant difference in the capital murder rate will be difficult to detect by even the most powerful statistical techniques. Yet the deterrent effect may be real—and the state is entitled to take the measures necessary to save the several lives that would be lost in the absence of the death penalty. A "small" saving in human life is not so insignificant or immaterial that it can be brushed aside as a permissible basis for legislative judgment.

In sum, although the evidence supporting the logical position that the death penalty deters capital crimes more effectively than life imprisonment is not yet conclusive, the evidence that there is no deterrent value will never be, and indeed cannot ever be, conclusive. The debate will persist unless and until the evidence of deterrence becomes conclusive, a possibility not to be ruled out. And so long as rational men can debate whether the death penalty deters crime, legislatures should be allowed to resolve that question for themselves and to act upon their decision free from interference by a judicial body that is neither well situated to collect and sift facts nor charged by the Constitution with that task. "[I]n passing on the validity of [legislation], it is not the province of a court to hear and examine evidence for the purpose of deciding again a question which the legislature has already decided. Its function is only to determine whether it is possible to say that the legislative decision is without rational basis. . . . [W]here, as here, the evidence . . . shows that it is at least a debatable question . . ., decision if for the legislature and not the courts." *Clark v. Paul Gray, Inc.*, 306 U.S. 583, 594. Congress and 35 states have resolved the debate in favor of capital punishment. . . .

Petitioners contend that Professor Ehrlich's study of the deterrent effect of capital punishment is open to criticism and consequently should be disregarded by the Court. For the reasons we discuss in the text, we believe that legislatures rather than courts must evaluate the technical merits of empirical studies. We have included this brief discussion of the merits of the debate between Professor Ehrlich and his critics only because of the vehemence of the assault upon his conclusions.

Petitioners have provided the Court with two technical discussions of Ehrlich's work (Jurek Pet. Br. App. 2, Sub-apps. C and E). The first is unsigned and the second is an unpublished paper by Passell and Taylor, "The Deterrent Effect of Capital Punishment: Another View" (hereafter Passell & Taylor). Two other criticisms of Ehrlich's work have been published. See Baldus and Cole, "A Comparison of the Work of Thorsten Sellin and Isaac Ehrlich on the Deterrent Effect of Capital Punishment," 85 *Yale Law Journal* 170 (1975) (hereafter Baldus & Cole); Bowers and Pierce, "The Illusion of Deterrence in Isaac Ehrlich's Research on Capital Punishment," 85 *Yale Law Journal* 187 (1975) (hereafter Bowers & Pierce). Both of these articles conclude that Ehrlich has overestimated the deterrent effects of capital punishment. Ehrlich's work also has been criticized by Yunker, "The Deterrent Effect of Capital Punishment: Comment" (hereafter Yunker), which concludes that errors in Ehrlich's study produce a five-fold underestimation in the deterrent effect. Ehrlich has responded to most of these criticisms in Ehrlich, "Deterrence: Evidence and Inference," 85 *Yale Law Journal* 209 (1975) (hereafter Ehrlich's reply). Jon K. Peck, an assistant professor of economics at Yale, agrees in part with Ehrlich and in part with his critics. Peck, "The Deterrent Effect of Capital Punishment: Ehrlich and His Critics," 85 *Yale Law Journal* 359 (1976) (hereafter Peck).

Ehrlich's critics have made four major arguments that, they contend, undercut the force of his conclusions. First, they argue that multiple regression analysis is unreliable. Second, they contend that Ehrlich used deficient data. Third, they believe that Ehrlich should not have included the post-1960 years in his study. Finally, they challenge Ehrlich's use of a logarithmic specification for some of his equations. We discuss these arguments in turn.

1. Petitioners contend (Jurek Pet. Br. App. 2, Sub-app. C)

199

that Professor Ehrlich's conclusions should be disregarded because "regression analysis is an exceptionally brittle tool of limited usefulness if conditions make it impossible to validate regression results with controlled experimentation" (*ibid.* at 2-44; footnote omitted). It is not possible to perform "controlled experimentation" on the death penalty; therefore, the argument concludes, regression analysis is "especially dangerous" (*ibid.*). See also Baldus & Cole.

We do not dispute the observation that linear regression analysis is quite sensitive to the identification of the potentially explaining factors that are thought to be the independent variables and to the specification of the mathematical relationship among them. Great care must be taken both to identify all of the relevant variables (in this case, all of the potential causes of a change in the murder rate) and to ensure that the apparently "independent" variables explain the dependent variable (murder) rather than each other. It is often difficult to achieve a certain explanation in the absence of "experimental" evidence, because only with a number of test sets of data to explore is it possible to reject with complete confidence a spurious covariance between the observed changes in the independent and dependent variables.

It is sometimes possible, however, to verify regression results by using the same specification to attempt to explain subsets of the available data. Professor Ehrlich has done so and reports that these results confirm his original findings. Ehrlich's reply, 85 *Yale Law Journal* at 217. Bowers & Pierce applied Ehrlich's method to a slightly different data base and obtained results similar to Ehrlich's, also confirming Ehrlich's original findings. Bowers & Pierce, 85 *Yale Law Journal* at 196; Ehrlich's reply, 85 *Yale Law Journal* at 210.

Moreover, in evaluating the weight to be given to findings of linear regression analysis, it is necessary to consider not only the pitfalls of the linear regression but also the defects of alternative methods. All things considered, it is the consensus of statisticians and econometricians that regression analysis is the most powerful statistical tool available for testing and evaluating competing explanations of observed variance in specific events. See generally Wonnacott and Wonnacott, *Econometrics* 1-9 (1972); Eaton, *Multivariate Statistical Analysis* (1972);

Snedecor and Cochran, *Statistical Methods* (6th ed. 1967); Ezekiel and Fox, *Methods of Correlation and Regression Analysis* (3d ed. 1959); Draper and Smith, *Applied Regression Analysis* (1966). It is the statistical method of choice whenever there are enough observations to make its use feasible. See also Finkelstein, "Regression Models in Administrative Proceedings," 86 *Harvard Law Review* 1442 (1973); Note, "Beyond the Prima Facie Case in Employment Discrimination Law: Statistical Proof and Rebuttal," 89 *Harvard Law Review* 387 (1975) (collecting cases).

Alternative methods, such as the "matched pairs of states" method advocated by Sellin, produce results that are completely unreliable. See the analysis of these methods at pages 39–43 of our brief. See also Ehrlich's reply, 85 *Yale Law Journal* at 222–224; Peck, 85 *Yale Law Journal* at 364–365 ("The matching approach has its own set of difficulties. It imposes relatively little explicit structure on the problem and is perhaps less likely than the econometric approach to find effects which are weak. The fundamental problem, however, is that the data are not generated in a controlled experiment. In making matched pairwise comparisons, the choice of pairs is inevitably subjective. . . . Even if states are correctly matched in terms of the averages of all relevant variables, other differences may be important. For example, of two states with the same average permanent income, one may have a much greater proportion of low income families than the other. If low income families were disproportionately responsible for homicides, the pairing of the two would be inappropriate. . . . A final difficulty is the possible response of punishment policies to homicide rates. For example, if high or rising homicide rates led states to institute the death penalty and low or declining rates led states to abolish the penalty, retentionist states would tend to have higher homicide rates. . . . The paired-comparison approach cannot adequately separate [all of the competing] effects, and consequently could fail to yield evidence of an underlying deterrent relationship.") Only regression analysis is capable of isolating the effects of a large number of variables, all of which may make some contribution to the murder rate. Only after that has been done is it possible to determine what role the death penalty plays in influencing the number of serious crimes. Re-

201

gression analysis must be used with care, but it, unlike the paired-state method, is at least capable of providing a meaningful answer if properly applied.

2. Bowers & Pierce (and, to some extent, the other critics) argue that Ehrlich has used inadequate data, and therefore that his results are open to question. They point out that the early years of data collected by the Uniform Crime Reporting System are not accurate (Bowers & Pierce, 85 *Yale Law Journal* at 187–192).

This criticism is, to a point, well taken. The data from the 1930s and 1940s are not entirely reliable, as the Uniform Crime Reports expressly concede. But this argument also discredits the earlier studies that do not find a deterrent effect. Although many of those studies relied upon data sources other than the Uniform Crime Reporting System, those sources, too, are not fully accurate. In addition, reliance on them would lead to errors of a different sort. The Census Bureau Vital Statistics data, for example, aggregates all homicides, while the Uniform Code data separates willful felonious homicides (which are likely to be capital crimes) from negligent manslaughters (which are not). See generally Ehrlich's reply, 85 *Yale Law Journal* at 212–214. What is more, any random errors in the data from the 1930s and 1940s would, in all likelihood, produce an underestimation in the deterrent value of capital punishment. See Ehrlich's reply, 85 *Yale Law Journal* at 213; Peck, 85 *Yale Law Journal* at 366; Ehrlich, "Rejoinder," 85 *Yale Law Journal* 368 (1976).

3. Passell & Taylor and Bowers & Pierce contend that Ehrlich should not have included the post-1960 years in his observations. They argue that if those years are deleted from the study the estimated deterrent effect disappears; they suggest that whenever a regression analysis spans a large number of years, there is a risk that social changes during those years will affect the relationship among the variables, so that the factors explaining murder committed at the beginning of the period will not do so (or will do so in a different way) at the end of the period.

This argument is not without its force. Yunker, too, argues that social changes in the 1950s make a continuous analysis inappropriate. But, as Yunker points out, if the 1960s are studied in isolation, a rapid decrease in the number of executions actually carried out is associated with a rapid increase in the murder rate. A study of that period alone led Yunker to conclude that each execution may have deterred 50 murders.

As Peck indicates (85 *Yale Law Journal* at 367, n. 27) Ehrlich probably would disagree with Yunker, just as he has disagreed with Sellin and with Bowers & Pierce. Ehrlich has argued that the inclusion of the 1960s in his study was necessary for two reasons: to obtain a sample of executions and murders of sufficient size that a statistical study yields reliable results, and to include a number of years when the execution rate was changing rapidly. Ehrlich's reply, 85 *Yale Law Journal* at 214–217. Because the execution and murder rates were either stable or changing only slowly in the 1930s and 1940s, a regression performed upon those decades alone would not have been reliable.

There are alternative explanations for the sudden surge in the number of murders in the 1960s. In one explanation, favored by Ehrlich and Yunker, the decrease in the number of executions plays some role. In the other, favored by Bowers & Pierce, changes in other social factors are so extensive they alone produce the increase. Professor Peck believes that we cannot know who is right until studies are performed on "disaggregated" data—studies for individual states, for particular spans of years different from those used by Ehrlich, and so on. Those studies are now under way.

4. Ehrlich used a logarithmic format for some of his calculations. Baldus & Cole, Bowers & Pierce, and Passell & Taylor all contend that if Ehrlich had used natural numbers his analysis would not have demonstrated a deterrent effect for the death penalty. This is primarily so, the critics explain, because in a logarithmic format the effect of reducing the execution rate close to zero in some years is given a disproportionate weight. Passell & Taylor attempted to duplicate Ehrlich's results with natural numbers and found no observable deterrent.

On the other hand, Yunker used natural numbers and estimated a deterrent effect much larger than that estimated by Ehrlich. Ehrlich himself contends (Ehrlich's reply, 85 *Yale Law Journal* at 217–219) that use of the logarithmic format was preferable for various reasons too technical to be explained here; moreover, he argues, he has performed regressions using natural numbers and has observed a deterrent effect. He attributes the contrary conclusions of Bowers & Pierce, and of Passell & Taylor, to basic statistical errors. Ehrlich's reply, 85 *Yale Law Journal* at 219–221, 225, n. 48. Peck agrees with Ehrlich that his critics have committed basic statistical errors (Peck, 85 *Yale Law Journal* at 367) and observes that neither the logarithmic form nor the natural number form "is likely to be exactly right, but only an approximately correct shape for the function is needed" (*ibid.* at 361). Once more, Peck suggests that additional work is necessary before we can know whether Ehrlich or his critics have the better of the argument.

Notes

1. There is strong empirical evidence that the threat of imprisonment deters crime (including murder) and that longer sentences are a more effective deterrent. See Ehrlich, "Participation in Illegitimate Activities: A Theoretical and Empirical Investigation," 81 *Journal of Political Economy* 521 (1973); Block and Lind, "An Economic Analysis of Crimes Punishable by Imprisonment," 4 *Journal of Legal Studies* 479 (1975); Ehrlich, "The Deterrent Effect of Criminal Law Enforcement," 1 *Journal of Legal Studies* 259 (1972); Gibbs, "Crime, Punishment, and Deterrence," 48 *Southwestern Social Science Quarterly* 515 (1968). Other studies are collected in van den Haag, *Punishing Criminals* 130–142 (1975).
2. Cf. Holmes, "The Path of the Law," 10 *Harvard Law Review* 457, 458–459 (1897) (it is the "bad man" whom the law regards as "normal," for only when a man is "bad" must the law depend on its threats of pain to change his behavior).
3. The Supreme Judicial Court of Massachusetts recently struck down under the Massachusetts constitution a pre-*Furman* death penalty statute. *Commonwealth v. O'Neal*, 339 N.E. 2d 676. The justices divided four to three on the constitutional question. Two of the four justices in the majority expressly noted that capital punishment might well be constitutional for carefully described categories of clearly deterrable crimes. See 339 N.E.2d at 694 (Hennessey, J., concurring); *ibid.* at 695 (Wilkins, J., concurring).
4. This paper is a revised and shortened version of Ehrlich, "The Deterrent Effect of Capital Punishment: A Question of Life and Death," 18 *National Bureau of Economic Research Working Papers* (November 1973), which we lodged with the Court in connection with *Fowler v. North Carolina*, No. 73-7031.

5. In fact, of the nine pairs of contiguous states studies by Bowers, eight pairs included a "death penalty state" that was *de facto* abolitionist. Bowers, *Executions in America* 137–163 (1974).
6. Commentators frequently have explained why the statistical material on the death penalty's deterrent value has until now been inconclusive. See, e.g., S. Rep. No. 93-721, 93d Cong., 1st Sess. 8–11 (1974); Royal Commission on Capital Punishment, *supra*, at pars. 62–67; 2 *Working Papers of the National Commission on Reform of the Federal Criminal Laws* 1354 (1970); Gibbs, "Crime, Punishment, and Deterrence," 48 *Southwestern Social Science Quarterly* 515 (1968); Hart, "Murder and the Principles of Punishment: England and the United States," 52 *Northwestern University Law Review* 433, 457 (1957).
7. In any event, we do not think that the meaning of the Eighth Amendment should turn on the results of the latest social science research. Neither should it turn on the secular trend in the murder rate, although it could be argued that, if the Court declared the death penalty unconstitutional and the murder rate increased, the increase would be evidence that a deterrent had been removed, and hence that the death penalty would again be constitutional. The alternative, that society would have to accept a higher murder rate because of a mistaken empirical estimate by the judiciary, seems unacceptable.
8. Approximately 20,600 murders were committed in 1974. Uniform Crime Reports of the Federal Bureau of Investigation, *Crime in the United States 1974*, pp. 15–19 (1975). Of course, not all of these murders were defined as capital crimes. There are no accurate data indicating the number of capital crimes committed each year.

Capital Punishment Is Not Imposed on the Basis of Race

The selection of those to be executed might be open to serious question if it were influenced by the race of the defendant. We submit that the data do not show that race is a factor.[1] We have included in . . . this brief an analysis of the findings of the studies relied upon by petitioners and others. These studies contradict each other, and the most recent (and sophisticated) study, the Stanford Note ("A Study of the California Penalty Jury in First-Degree-Murder Cases: Standardless Sentencing," 21 *Stanford Law Review* 1297 (1969)), found no evidence whatever of racial discrimination in capital punishment for murder. We are aware of no properly conducted study that supports a contrary conclusion.

The only studies that even inferentially suggest a possibility of racial discrimination were conducted in the South during a time when blacks were often excluded from grand and petit juries. They do not demonstrate that discrimination persists now that blacks sit in judgment on other blacks. It is true that both the National Prisoner Statistics (Law Enforcement Assistance

Administration, *Capital Punishment 1974*, Table 16 (1975))
and information compiled by the NAACP (Jurek Pet. Br. 83–84,
n.147) indicate that approximately 50 to 60 percent of all those
sentenced to death are black. This is only the beginning of the
inquiry, however. In order to determine whether this indicates
discrimination, we would need to know what proportion of all
capital crimes are committed by blacks.[2] Although there is no
direct measure of that proportion, the number of arrests for
willful felonious homicide may be the closest approximation.
The Uniform Crime Reports of the Federal Bureau of Investigation (*Crime in the United States 1974*, p. 191 (1975)) indicate
that 57.1 percent of those arrested for willful felonious homicides are black. There is, therefore, little or no discernable discrimination against blacks from the time of arrest through the
pronouncement of a sentence of death; blacks are not a higher
proportion of those sentenced to die than they are of those arrested for the most serious types of murder.[3] Nor is there any
evidence that blacks are arrested for their crimes more often
than are whites. The evidence concerning arrest is consistent
with the evidence concerning the race of the victim. Exactly
half of all murder victims are black. *Crime in the United States
1974*, p. 15 (1975). If capital punishment deters murders (as legislatures are entitled to conclude), it would follow that abolition of capital punishment would work to the detriment of the
poor and the blacks, who are disproportionately the victims of
murder.

If it is proper to assume that some individuals in the criminal-justice system discriminate on account of race or other impermissible factors, the existence or extent of this discrimination will vary from time to time, place to place, and state to
state. Proof of discrimination by the prosecutor and juries of
one county in one state would not prove that petitioners in
these five cases are the objects of discrimination. It is unlikely
that discrimination can account for the sentences imposed
upon petitioners Gregg, Jurek, and Proffitt, who are white. The
argument that blacks may be treated harshly when they have
committed crimes against whites is not an argument against the
penalty imposed upon a black who murders another black, as
was the case in *Fowler*.

In short, the possibility of racial discrimination in the selection or imposition of a particular punishment depends strictly upon the facts and circumstances of the case. It is not an argument against all capital punishment for all time. Indeed, the argument has nothing whatever to do with capital punishment. Any punishment selected or augmented on racial grounds is impermissible. No petitioner has contended that he was discriminated against on account of his race. Accordingly, the possibility that racial discrimination exists upon occasion in the criminal-justice system is not an argument against the penalty imposed upon petitioners.

Petitioner in *Fowler* relied (Pet. Br. 136, n. 226) upon what he asserted are "discrete and limited but careful studies" demonstrating racial discrimination in the imposition of capital punishment. Petitioner Jurek joins this assertion and relies upon one additional study (*Jurek* Pet. Br. 81–84, nn. 146–147). Petitioner Roberts, although not relying upon the authorities cited in *Fowler,* also contends that there is racial discrimination (*Roberts* Pet. Br. 69).

Most of the studies relied upon reflect experience in southern states during a time when blacks often were excluded from grand and petit juries. Whatever force they may have is diminished by this simple fact. One study finds racial discrimination in rape cases alone. And one study relied upon by petitioners finds *no* evidence of racial discrimination. We examine the studies below.

1. Johnson, "The Negro and Crime," 217 *Annals* 93 (1941). Johnson studied the imposition of death sentences in Richmond, Virginia between 1930 and 1939, five counties in North Carolina between 1930 and 1940, and Fulton County, Georgia between February 1938 and September 1939. The Georgia study was fruitless because of insufficient data. In Richmond only one sentence of death was imposed—on a white man. In the North Carolina sample 218 blacks were convicted of murder and 17 (or 7.8%) of them were sentenced to death; 44 whites were convicted of murder and 8 (or 18%) of them were sentenced to death. Of those convicted, whites were therefore more likely to be sentenced to death than blacks. Of those sentenced to death, 71.6% of the blacks and 69% of the whites were executed; the difference is not statistically significant. Al-

though blacks appeared to be convicted more often than whites, it was not possible within the scope of the study to determine whether this difference was attributable to race, to the nature and frequency of crimes committed, or to other factors. Johnson himself observed that his data were not conclusive.

2. Garfinkel, "Research Note on Inter- and Intra-Racial Homicides," 27 *Social Forces* 369 (1949). Garfinkel collected data from 10 counties in North Carolina between 1930 and 1940. The study attempted to detect any difference in the penalty assessed for inter-racial murders as opposed to that assessed for intra-racial murders. His data cut two ways: a white convicted of murdering one of his own race was *more* likely (18.6%) than a black convicted of murdering one of his own race (6.7%) to be sentenced to death, while a black convicted of murdering a white was more likely (42.9%) to be sentenced to death than was a white convicted of murdering a black (0%). The net effect of this is unclear, and Garfinkel declined to engage in "sheer speculation" about it (27 *Social Forces* at 381).

3. Johnson, "Selective Factors in Capital Punishment," 36 *Social Forces* 165 (1957). This is not a "study" at all, but simply is a listing of the persons convicted of capital offenses in North Carolina since 1909. The author asserts that race is an important factor because 73.8% of those sentenced to death are black. He acknowledges, however, that this phenomenon could as easily be explained by differences in the rate in which individuals commit capital crimes (blacks in North Carolina were more likely to be poor, and the poor are more likely to commit violent offenses). Johnson observes that the more recent figures (the 1950s, in his study) reveal a narrowing in the difference between the rate at which the races are sentenced to death.

4. Wolfgang, Kelly & Nolde, "Comparison of the Executed and the Commuted among Admissions to Death Row," 53 *Journal of Criminal Law, Criminology & Police Science* 301 (1962). This study concludes that the death sentences of whites are slightly more likely to be commuted than are the sentences of blacks. [This is inconsistent with the results reported in the Johnson study at 217 *Annals, supra.*] However, the authors did not assess the effect of prior criminal record upon the commutation rate, and, if Bedau's study (*infra*) is correct, many apparently racial differences can be explained by differences in the

209

number of prior criminal convictions of those sentenced to death. The authors concede that "too many unknown or presently immeasurable factors prevent our making definitive statements about the relationship" between race and execution rates.

5. Bedau, "Death Sentences in New Jersey 1907–1960," 19 *Rutgers Law Review* 1 (1964). Bedau analyzed the death sentence in New Jersey using data from 1907 to 1960. He concluded: (1) Because data establish that blacks commit three to six times as many capital crimes per individual as do whites, no discrimination would be established unless (in New Jersey) more than 65% of all those executed were black. The actual rate of black executions was discovered to be less than this, and, consequently, discrimination was not proved. (2) The only arguable evidence of discrimination was the fact that 17.7% of the whites sentenced to death had their sentences commuted, while only 8.1% of the blacks so sentenced were granted a commutation. Bedau also found, however that this difference becomes statistically insignificant if past criminal record of the offender is accounted for. The author concludes: "No evidence has been found, and no inferences have been drawn from the facts as reported in the course of this study that racial prejudice in the courts or commutation authority has been a proximate cause of the evident differential treatment accorded non-whites under sentence of death" (19 *Rutgers Law Review* at 53).

6. Wolfgang and Reidel, "Race, Jury Discretion, and the Death Penalty," 407 *Annals* 119 (1973). The authors report on a comprehensive study, sponsored by the NAACP, of rape convictions in 11 southern states between 1945 and 1965. The data revealed that among all those convicted of rape, blacks were selected disproportionately for the death sentence. Thirteen percent of all blacks convicted of rape were sentenced to death; two percent of all whites convicted were so sentenced. The study carefully isolated the effects of the age and prior record of the offender, and of numerous characteristics of the victim, offense, and trial. Even after controlling for these effects a substantial portion of the disparity in sentencing was attributable to race. This is a careful and comprehensive study, and we do not question its conclusion that during the 20 years in question, in southern states, there was discrimination in rape cases. See

also Wolfgang, "Racial Discrimination in the Death Sentence for Rape," in *Executions in America* 114 (Bowers ed. 1974) (reporting on the same research). The research does not provide support for a conclusion that racial discrimination continues, however, or that it applies to murder cases.

7. Petitioner Roberts refers (*Roberts* Pet. Br. 69) to Professor Wolfgang's assertion that "[t]he evidence of racial discrimination in capital punishment in twentieth century America is . . . hardly contestable." Wolfgang, "Racial Discrimination in the Death Sentence for Rape," in *Executions in America* 114, 117 (Bowers ed. 1974). As we have indicated above, the evidence upon which Professor Wolfgang relies relates to rape cases in the south during a period when blacks often were excluded from grand and petit juries. To the extent the assertion is meant to have a broader meaning, it is a statement exceeding the scope of the study.

8. Some have cited Koeninger, *Capital Punishment in Texas, 1924–1968* 123 (1969), as a study demonstrating that capital punishment is imposed discriminatorily. Koeninger obtained the available records on 483 Texas cases. He observed that blacks are sentenced to death in disproportionate numbers, and concluded that this indicates racial discrimination. He made no attempt to discover whether this disparity could have been caused by differences in the rate at which capital crimes are committed, and he did not attempt to control for the effects of other variables, such as prior record of the offenders. This study therefore is an inference of discrimination directly from the fact that approximately half of those executed are black. For the reasons we [have discussed earlier], inferences of this sort are meaningless. A similar problem infects the conclusions of those authors who have inferred discrimination directly from the reported execution data without performing any independent studies. See Alexander, "The Abolition of Capital Punishment," *Proceedings of the 96th Congress of Correction of the American Correctional Association*, Baltimore, Maryland 57, 59 (1966); Williams, "The Death Penalty and the Negro," 67 *The Crisis* 501 (1960); Hartung, "Trends in the Use of Capital Punishment," 284 *Annals* 8, 14–17 (1952); Hochkammer, "The Capital Punishment Controversy," 60 *Journal of Criminal Law, Criminology & Police Science* 360, 362 (1969).

9. Petitioner Jurek relies upon the assertion of petitioner Fowler (*Fowler* Pet. Br. 136, n. 226) that "it has *seemed apparent* to responsible commissions and individuals studying the administration of the death penalty in this country [that there is discrimination on account of race.]" The responsible individuals to whom this "seemed apparent" conducted no independent research; each of the authorities relied upon what is apparently the received wisdom that discrimination exists. See The President's Commission on Law Enforcement and the Administration of Justice, *The Challenge of Crime in a Free Society* 143 (1967); Clark, *Crime in America* 335 (1970). But, as the discussion of the statistical studies cited by petitioners should make clear, the received wisdom is not supported by the data and is open to serious question. The most recent (and most sophisticated) study found no evidence of discrimination in murder cases. Note, "A Study of the California Penalty Jury in First-Degree-Murder Cases: Standardless Sentencing," 21 *Stanford Law Review* 1297, 1346, 1366–1367, 1417–1420 (1969). See also the data collected in respondent's brief in *Aikens v. California*, No. 68–5027, October Term, 1971, pages 105–108, which demonstrates that although blacks received 18.6% of the death sentences in California, they were the beneficiaries of 25% of the commutations.

After summarizing most of the studies conducted through 1973, Professor Bowers, an opponent of capital punishment, concluded (Bowers, *Executions in America* 74–75 (1974)): "There are obvious shortcomings in the body of research. The studies are regionally and historically selective. Most states with the death penalty have not been included in any of these investigations . . . Furthermore, . . . most have failed to test the independence of the racial differences they have uncovered." We agree with this assessment. But we also agree with Hochkammer, *supra*, 60 *Journal of Criminal Law, Criminology & Police Science* at 362, that even if discrimination were proven, "it would be a mistake to argue that capital punishment should be rejected because some discrimination exists. The proper approach is to remedy the defect, not abolish the system."

Notes

1. See also *Furman v. Georgia, supra,* 408 U.S. at 389–390, n.12 (Burger, C. J., dissenting); *ibid.* at 310, n.14 (Stewart, J., concurring); *ibid.* at 447 (Powell, J., dissenting).
2. "These statistics alone, of course, do not reveal elements of judicial bias in the administration of criminal law. It is also well recognized that blacks in American society . . . have a criminal homicide rate that is between four and ten times greater than that of whites." Wolfgang and Riedel, "Race, Judicial Discretion, and the Death Penalty," 407 *Annals* 119, 123 (1973). See also White, "The Role of the Social Sciences in Determining the Constitutionality of Capital Punishment," 13 *Duquesne Law Review* 279, 281–285 (1974).
3. Many murders or other capital crimes grow out of other violent felonies. The Uniform Crime Reports indicate that blacks are arrested for these crimes, too, in disproportionate numbers. Of those arrested for robbery 62.3 percent are black; of those arrested for aggravated assault 41.2 percent are black. *Crime in the United States 1974,* p. 191 (1975).

Index

215

216

218

219

221